Building Effective Development in Elementary School

Learn the principles of comprehensive professional development and motivate elementary school teachers to be more effective in the classroom! In *Building Effective Professional Development in Elementary School,* Judy Johnson presents a career-long and comprehensive approach to professional development that gives teachers the support they need to improve instruction and raise the levels of student achievement. Her book not only explains how to create and lead a successful PD program, it also offers practical advice for establishing a school culture that will encourage teachers to collaborate and self-motivate in an effort to improve instruction. Other topics include:

- Training to deepen content knowledge and expand the teaching repertoire;
- Identifying high-performing educators and helping them build upon their strengths;
- Using teaching demonstrations to enliven and diversify classroom practice;
- Creating an effective mentorship program that brings out the best in faculty members, regardless of experience level;
- Resolving problems with recruitment, dealing with disgruntled teachers, assessing teaching quality, and overcoming other obstacles preventing implementation of a comprehensive professional development program;
- And more!

Judy Johnson is a consultant and former teacher. She served as executive director of the Cotsen Foundation for the Art of Teaching in Los Angeles, CA, from 2001 to 2013. Prior to that role, she was vice president of the Los Angeles Education Partnership, where she directed all programs, including the professional development of K-12 teachers.

Also Available from Eye On Education

(www.routledge.com/eyeoneducation)

Easy and Effective Professional Development:
The Power of Observation to Improve Teaching
Catherine Beck, Paul D'Elia, and Michael W. Lamond

Making Good Teaching Great:
Everyday Strategies for Teaching with Impact
Todd Whitaker and Annette Breaux

Leading Schools in an Era of Declining Resources
J. Howard Johnston and Ronald Williamson

Creating Safe Schools:
A Guide for School Leaders, Teachers, and Parents
Franklin P. Schargel

The School Leader's Guide to Formative Assessment:
Using Data to Improve Student and Teacher Achievement
Todd Stanley and Jana Alig

Informal Classroom Observations on the Go:
Feedback, Discussion, and Reflection
Sally J. Zepeda

Professional Development:
What Works, Second Edition
Sally J. Zepeda

Building Effective Professional Development in Elementary School

Designing a Path to Excellent Teaching

Judy Johnson

Routledge
Taylor & Francis Group

NEW YORK AND LONDON

First published 2018
by Routledge
711 Third Avenue, New York, NY 10017

and by Routledge
2 Park Square, Milton Park, Abingdon, Oxon, OX14 4RN

Routledge is an imprint of the Taylor & Francis Group, an informa business

© 2018 Taylor & Francis

Library of Congress Cataloging-in-Publication Data
A catalog record for this book has been requested.

ISBN: 978-1-138-57769-5 (hbk)
ISBN: 978-1-138-57770-1 (pbk)
ISBN: 978-1-351-26628-4 (ebk)

Typeset in Palatino
by Apex CoVantage, LLC

This book is dedicated to Lloyd E. Cotsen, who believed in the power of teachers to change children's lives by instilling in them a lifelong love of learning. This book is also dedicated to all teachers who continuously aspire to be the best educators they can be and who work diligently to achieve success with each of their students.

Contents

Author's Note

The names of the students in this book have been changed to respect their privacy.

Acknowledgments

This book stems from more than 15 years of work on the development of gifted teaching by the Cotsen Foundation for the Art of Teaching. I want to thank the 1,000 plus teachers and administrators who helped us identify and build upon new and exciting ways that teachers learn to become exceptional at their craft. I am deeply grateful to the foundation's board of directors who have so fully supported the work: Margit Cotsen, Margaret Funkhouser, Gary Hart, Steven Koblik, Steve Lavine, Lucia Laguarda, Barry Munitz, and Jonathan Victor. I am indebted, of course, to the staff of the foundation for their tireless efforts to implement our program, their insights, and the time they spent collecting information for this book, especially Angela Bae, Lyndon Catayong, Isaac Cox, Dana Farahani, Vivian Galanti, Dianne Glinos, Barbara Golding, Jerry Harris, Greg Nicholson, and Tyler Sanders.

We have been fortunate to collaborate with many individuals involved in educational research and nonprofit organizations in our efforts to provide opportunities for experienced teachers to aspire to achieve greatness in their teaching and their students' learning outcomes. In addition to people specifically named in the book, I am grateful for the ideas and introductions to teacher leaders offered by Susan Empson, Megan Franke, Vicki Jacobs, and Angela Chan Turrou.

Friends and colleagues willing to give honest feedback, along with encouragement to continue, proved invaluable. They include Margit Cotsen, John McDonald, Diana McDonough, Mike Rose, Judy Shane, and Lana Spitz. I am grateful to my editor, Lauren Davis, for her creative thinking and practical suggestions as she shepherded this project through the publishing process. Finally, special thanks go to my husband, Anthony Krulic, who has been a critical reader, careful editor, and my most vocal cheerleader.

Introduction

The more I learn about teaching, and about people and students, I feel like I know so little. That makes me want to know more and it makes me curious. It makes me a better person, I think. I approach things differently, so that I can get some sort of result from it. I just keep going. I want to sit on the shoulders of giants and become just as good . . . just as great. I choose my mentors and I model after them. I want to be better, whether personally or professionally.

(Cindy Bak, teacher in Rowland Unified School District)

How can I be a better teacher and how can I be more effective for my students and for myself? It starts with the teacher and figuring out, "What do you want to get out of teaching? What do I want to leave behind?" It comes down to "It's not just one year of teaching" but it's "What's your legacy?" "What do I want to leave behind for my students and my colleagues?"

(Carlen LeHessinger, teacher, Rowland Unified School District)

It's like what Maya Angelou said, "When you know better, you do better." From my experience, I can say that I thought I was a good teacher, but perhaps I was focused on the wrong things. Taking a step back and appreciating the art of teaching, the humanity of the kids, and just how much we influence their lives, helps me to stay focused on their learning, foremost, and their enjoyment, and making sure that they want to learn. I make a conscious effort to bring them resources and activities that hopefully will influence their lives.

(Araceli Nunez-Tallman, teacher in Long Beach Unified School District)

When I hear these teachers speak about their craft, I sense their drive to perfect their work and their commitment to creating a better future for children. This is a book about effective professional development, but is also a story about what motivates teachers to achieve their best and strive for excellence.

New teachers generally enter the profession eager to learn more about how to teach children successfully. Like most human beings, they have an inherent tendency to seek out challenge, to explore, and to learn (Pink 2009, 8). Sadly, after an induction phase, these novices usually find themselves isolated and left on their own to figure out how children learn best. The professional learning opportunities available to them often fail to provide what they need to expand their repertoire of teaching skills and become truly artful educators. Teachers want to feel a strong sense of purpose in what they are learning and in their work. They need to sense that they are getting better at teaching. While wanting some autonomy so that they can choose for themselves how and when to improve, they also enjoy and can benefit from a feeling of camaraderie as they work to accomplish their purpose (Fullan 2011, 4). These characteristics should all be embedded into their professional development. This book explores various ways to enable educators to become both expert and more successful at their calling.

Can teachers learn to be great, or are the gifted ones simply naturals born to the profession? This book stems from a quest to answer that question. In a program called the Art of Teaching, we attempted to determine whether, when given a nurturing environment and appropriate support, competent teachers change and grow; and secondly, what specific support they need to help them perfect their craft. Our evidence in working with many teachers has convinced me that they can and do learn to become highly competent, and many even achieve exceptional levels of skill.

Unfortunately, the professional development most often offered to teachers is not focused on continuous improvement or designed to help educators attain excellence. The authors of *The Internal Coherence Framework: Creating the Conditions for Continuous Improvement in Schools* (Forman, Stosch, and Bochala 2017) discuss how to put ambitious teaching at the core of instruction. They describe systems in which the work of leadership and teaching teams is organized around the vision of improvement, the environment is psychologically safe for teams working together, and the culture of schools and the district supports the risk-taking and challenges necessary to move to higher levels of performance. While there is evidence of improvement in professional development offered, much more needs to change for it to be effective. A study of professional development available for U.S. teachers from 2000 through 2008 (Wei, Hammond, and Adamson 2010) revealed that the content teachers taught was progressively more the focus of professional development and more time was spent on this subject. At the same time, the intensity of learning sessions declined. Teachers had fewer experiences with eight or more hours of training than they did four years previously. Short-term workshops—the least effective model—was the format used most often for subjects such as reading, teaching English as a second language, or addressing the specific needs of special education students. While three-fourths of teachers say they have opportunities to collaborate on planning, they engaged in this for only 2.7 hours per week on average, and their work rarely led to the implementation of a cooperative school culture. Only 16 percent of teachers reported collaborative efforts in 2008 as compared to 2000 when 34 percent did so. Finally,

American teachers have far less time for cooperative work with colleagues as compared with educators in high-achieving OECD (Organization for Economic and Co-operative Development) nations. Current structures such as school schedules rarely permit U.S. teachers to engage in the deep study with colleagues that is essential to strengthening teaching and learning, though conditions do vary by state, and some states are making substantial progress in creating more supportive conditions for continuous improvement.

My purpose is to outline a path to success by elucidating lessons learned from elementary school educators that show how to get to great teaching and how to be artful in this profession. I also hope to elevate the expectations for what teachers can achieve with their students, and encourage a more widespread implementation of proven professional development practices that allow teachers at all stages of their careers to refine their practice to levels of excellence. Readers will find examples of great teaching in action. Interested school and district leaders will discover various techniques that help teachers continuously improve instruction and raise the levels of student achievement.

Why focus on elementary schools? The first few years of schooling are critical to the future success of children. During those years, students are expected to learn to read with fluency and acquire the foundational skills to manipulate numbers and calculate mathematical problems. In grades K-6, children in the U.S. learn the intricacies of the English language so that they can comprehend and communicate what they read, and learn to speak and write with clarity, interest, persuasion, and accuracy. Great teaching can generate a lifetime love of reading and learning. It instills in students a sense of confidence and a habit of persistence as they solve problems. What and how children are taught will speed or hinder their progress in the years to come. Great teaching lays the foundation for a promising academic future, so it is essential that elementary school teachers have the knowledge and training they need to achieve the best outcomes for these young people.

The quotations and teaching exemplars used in this book come primarily from my experience at the Cotsen Foundation for the Art of Teaching, which for more than 15 years has provided professional development to more than 1,000 teachers from 130 plus elementary schools and 25 school districts in California. Insights and information from the Art of Teaching have been gleaned from classroom observations, workshop presentations, teaching videos, annual surveys of teachers and administrators, speeches and newsletter articles written by teachers, and 32 individual interviews with participants.

Additional examples are drawn from descriptions of the Elementary Mathematics Laboratory Class at the University of Michigan, and from interviews with leaders of professional development programs in several states that center on the Cognitively Guided Instruction approach to mathematics. Teachers and administrators who describe their experiences come from a variety of school settings. The terrain includes schools embedded in small districts and others from large school systems; low-income and affluent neighborhoods; plus, some communities with large numbers of pupils for whom English is a second language. The stories shared by these educators illustrate how exceptional teaching can thrive in any community where the school and district administrators create a positive climate for continuous learning and provide the resources needed to keep that teaching improving.

What's Inside This Book?

Building Effective Professional Development in Elementary School identifies six steps along the path toward excellent teaching. It presents a career-long and comprehensive approach to professional development that can give teachers the support they need to improve instruction and become exceptionally effective in teaching their students. Each of these steps is covered in one of the first six chapters:

- ◆ *Chapter 1: Aspire to Achieve Excellence.* The first step along the path toward great teaching involves making a commitment to continuous improvement and raising expectations for what quality teaching can accomplish for students.
- ◆ *Chapter 2: Invest in the Best and Build upon Strengths.* Identifying high-performing educators and helping them build upon their strengths will prepare them to become teacher leaders who can more effectively assist others.
- ◆ *Chapter 3: Get a Vision: The Power of Observations.* Witnessing great teachers at work serves as an inspiration to learn more about pedagogy and student learning processes.
- ◆ *Chapter 4: Go Deep into Content and Methodology.* An effective professional development program designed to promote excellent teaching comes in a variety of formats and features choice, focus, intensity, duration, and practice.
- ◆ *Chapter 5: Practice with a Mentor–Coach.* As teachers try to implement new practices to which they have been introduced, they benefit greatly from the feedback, modeling, and encouragement a mentor can provide.

◆ *Chapter 6: Collaborate with Colleagues and Make Teaching Public.*
   Opening classrooms to share practices and solve problems with
   peers makes it possible for teachers to learn continuously from each
   other.
◆ *Chapter 7: Key Roles of School and District Leaders.* Principals and
   district leaders play essential roles in promoting continuous learning
   and providing appropriate professional development.
◆ *Chapter 8: Obstacles along the Way.* Potential problems that may arise
   as individual schools and districts implement a new and more
   effective kind of professional learning program can be avoided or
   overcome.
◆ *Chapter 9: Measures of Success.* A variety of measures must be used to
   assess whether instruction and student achievement are improving
   as more effective professional development practices are put in
   place.
◆ *Chapter 10: Looking toward the Future.* The influx of so many new
   teachers into schools makes this an opportune time to create
   collaborative school cultures to support teacher learning and
   contribute to the overall development of the teaching profession.

References

Forman, Michelle L., Elizabeth Leisy Stosch, and Candice Bocala. 2017.
   *The Internal Coherence Framework: Creating the Conditions for Continuous
   Improvement in Schools.* Cambridge, MA: Harvard Education Press.
Fullan, Michael. 2011. *Motivating the Masses: Experiencing is Believing.* Retrieved
   October 28, 2017 from http://michaelfullan.ca/wp-content/uploads/
   2016/06/13396086820.pdf.
Pink, Daniel H. 2009. *Drive: The Surprising Truth about What Motivates Us.* New
   York: Riverhead Books.
Wei, Ruth, Linda Darling Hammond, and Frank Adamson. 2010. *Professional
   Development in the United States: Trends and Challenges.* Dallas, TX and
   Stanford, CA: National Staff Development Council and Stanford Center
   for Opportunity Policy in Education.

1

Aspire to Achieve Excellence

Great teaching—do we know it when we see it? Surprisingly, the answer to this question is not always "yes." It turns out that conceptions of greatness can change as we witness more examples of excellence, as they can cause our expectations to rise. When the staff at the Art of Teaching began observing well-respected elementary school teachers at work, we were impressed with the organized, purposeful, challenging, and engaging instruction, to which the children responded enthusiastically. Certainly, these teachers demonstrated high levels of competence. Then, as we watched more lessons in classrooms and on video, we were thrilled to discover even more effective performances by teachers resulting in remarkable student achievement and a much deeper understanding of the subjects. The thoughtful and targeted teaching of so many lessons produced a level of student comprehension and skill that seemed almost hard to believe. In subsequent lessons, it became clear that these gifted teachers exhibited this top-notch level of teaching day in and day out. Truly inspiring teachers never stop looking for ways to reach every child in their care.

In developing a program to achieve higher quality teaching, the first step is to change one's mindset and reconsider what levels of achievement both teachers and students might reach. Most of us underestimate what children can learn and do. With the guidance of masterful instructors, youngsters flourish in unexpected ways. Because teachers and administrators get few opportunities to visit classrooms to see great teaching, their expectations for successful instruction are often as limited as ours were when we began our quest to identify the best instructors. We began to better understand the complexities of teaching after we watched dozens of gifted teachers in action and noticed the variety in those performances.

Great teaching is not a package of procedures and steps one can repeat. It comes in many forms and is shaped, in part, by the person doing the teaching. Each teacher brings his or her own style and personality to the performance. Some are extroverted and dramatic in their presentations. Others are quietly systematic. The best lessons are ones that suit each teacher's nature while challenging students and carrying them forward in their learning. When given the opportunity to observe a teacher in action, one should watch carefully how instruction affects the children in the class. What insights do students gain? What misconceptions are clarified? What skills are they developing over time? How do they see themselves as learners?

Lenses for Observation

Many things occur simultaneously during a classroom lesson and it can be difficult to focus on everything at once. We found it more beneficial to divide aspects of teaching into categories and look at one or two of them at a time. Within each category, which we dubbed a "lens for observation," we watched and extracted exemplary practices we had witnessed. We chose words such as "coherent," "challenging," "relevant," "clear," "cumulative," and "purposeful." These descriptors were particularly handy on occasions when we shared our findings with those who were not teachers. In a presentation sponsored by the Hechinger Institute at Columbia University, we presented videos of great teaching and introduced terminology to help journalists new to the education beat understand what to look for when they observe classroom instruction.

As these lenses led us to a deeper comprehension of the complexities of teaching, we also recognized a great variation in successful practices. Highly effective teachers continue to refine their practices over their entire careers. As they do, those of us who are privileged to watch them may find new dimensions to add to our understanding of excellent teaching.

Traditional Teaching Versus Artful Teaching

Imagine a classroom led by a competent teacher in a traditional, well-functioning school. Classes are orderly and relatively quiet. Teachers are in charge and do most of the talking and much of the work. Textbooks drive instruction and students use pre-developed worksheets for assignments. Teachers feel pressured by the school district's pacing guidelines and keep moving along whether the children have mastered the content or not. Students are expected to respond to the teacher's instructions, follow procedures, and copy the model the teacher presents.

Box 1.1   Lenses for Observation

Content

- ◆ Teaches to content standards and above
- ◆ Makes clear the teaching points and tasks
- ◆ Provides challenging, relevant, important material
- ◆ Chooses content level appropriate for each child
- ◆ Uses academic language
- ◆ Integrates more than one subject when appropriate

Instruction

- ◆ Is purposeful: Students know why they are learning the material
- ◆ Is coherent: Lesson is structured with a connected beginning, middle, end
- ◆ Accumulates and builds on prior learning
- ◆ Uses a variety of methods and materials
- ◆ Involves inquiry, choice, decision-making for students
- ◆ Engages children in conversation about their thinking
- ◆ Utilizes time well

Assessment

- ◆ Continuous checking for understanding in various ways

Social Environment

- ◆ Students add to others' learning
- ◆ Students do a lot of the work
- ◆ Students demonstrate positive interactions with teacher and each other

Physical Environment

- ◆ Is attractive, safe, clean
- ◆ Allows easy access to materials giving students more independence
- ◆ Features student work around the room and uses it as models
- ◆ Includes teacher-designed materials posted for reference needs

Effects on Students

- ◆ Engaging actively
- ◆ Working productively
- ◆ Persisting with difficult tasks
- ◆ Contributing to classroom learning

Teaching to the whole class dominates, though small-group instruction may be interspersed for reading or math. Children are ability grouped early in the year and those placements seldom vary, even when individual students acquire new skills.

The environment is neat and attractive, with some student work posted on the walls along with ready-made teaching materials. Curriculum standards and lesson objectives specific to the grade level are written on the board and may be referenced by the teacher at the start of lessons. Lessons are frequently structured using an approach like the seven-step plan advocated by noted researcher and educator Madeline Hunter in the last half of the twentieth century. The sequence starts with review and goes on to include introducing a "hook" to capture student interest, stating the purpose and specific objective of the lesson, providing input, checking for understanding, offering guided practice, and having students work independently. While in theory, this structure for teaching seems sound, the quality and effectiveness of the teaching is dependent on how artfully the teacher embraces this framework. For example, following the seven-step plan, one teacher told her students that the purpose of the day's lesson was to prepare to do well on the upcoming language arts test and impress the principal with their performance. In contrast, a more accomplished instructor spelled out how understanding the structure of nonfiction texts can help them as a reader better comprehend the material and can also help the students improve their organization and writing of their own nonfiction essays or articles. The benefits described were not just temporary results on a test, but the development of skills they could use for the rest of their lives.

Now let's envision a school in which artful teaching prevails. We see many of the same characteristics of good instruction, but here the teaching is far more complex and nuanced. As in the traditional classrooms, procedures are in place for making students secure about what is expected of them. In an environment of artful teaching, however, transitions from one activity to another are swift, and time for instruction is used with greater efficiency. There is a purposeful feel about the teaching, like a fine-tuned locomotive keeping on track as it steadily progresses toward its destination. Still, the teacher may make a slight detour to take advantage of a spontaneous learning opportunity created by the ways children respond during the lesson.

Rooms are noisier, with students talking a great deal to each other and to the entire class. Through these conversations, they practice their language skills and clarify their thinking. Teachers push children not simply to state their answers, but also to explain how they arrived at their conclusions.

These responses give teachers a view into what the students understand about the task and what misconceptions remain. Students get specific praise for correct answers and for using different and useful approaches to finding solutions. Children are actively engaged for large portions of time doing the work along with the teacher, in groups, and by themselves. The teacher forms small groups of students who need to learn similar material, and then frequently changes those groups as students progress at varying rates.

As in other good classrooms, the environment is appealing. The emphasis here though is on efficient learning, not only visual attractiveness. Space is organized so that students have easy access to materials and supplies, promoting greater independence on their part. Teachers need not spend precious time doling out the equipment to children which they can reach themselves. The room also serves as a learning tool with instructor-made posters of teaching points and examples of how students may approach a task. Children refer to the materials while working on their own. Student work posted on the walls varies, illustrating many ways children have successfully tackled a math problem, analyzed a text, or written a story. Often, a collection of an individual child's work is posted to show how, with many revisions and persistence, the student eventually created a final product of higher quality.

Teaching is structured around curriculum standards, but frequently a single lesson includes multiple standards, with some above grade-level for children who are ready to move ahead in their performance. A lesson may focus on teaching all the students a specific concept, such as adding mixed fractions in a word problem, but children are asked to choose from different sets of numbers for the problem they will solve. Those who are prepared to work with more complex sets of numbers using the same concept can do so. Each student may also select the tools he or she will use to solve a problem. The children draw diagrams, use tally marks, play with counters or plastic cubes, count on their fingers, or make calculations in their heads before writing these procedures and equations down. In these ways, students learn the same principles in math, but every child can approach the specific task at the level of complexity each is prepared to handle.

While the structure of lessons may resemble those in other classrooms, more time in this class is generally devoted to students exploring the content independently. Lessons might be turned around so that students are given a task to do alone first. They confer with a partner about how each approached the work, and some students share with the class the different methods they used. Near the lesson's end, the teacher may summarize the concepts demonstrated by their examples.

Regardless of the grade level, the demand on students is greater in these rooms. They are expected to challenge themselves and push to achieve more. They are asked not only to be responsible for their own learning, but to contribute to the progressive understanding of their classmates. High expectations lead to surprising results. Exemplary teachers know that the children in their classes can think and perform far above the standards typically established in the past.

Examples of Artful Teaching

The following four examples offer a more detailed view of excellent teaching and include extended commentaries. Each illustrates rigorous instruction. In the first, we see the teacher nurturing kindergartners and presenting them with demanding learning tasks. She demonstrates what it means to "believe that every single child can learn and deserves to be challenged." In the second example, first-graders learn to become authors who can write lively sentences for their readers. Following that comes reading instruction for second-graders. The children learn both decoding skills and comprehension strategies. Continuous assessment and masterfully organized small-group instruction contribute to the success of students. In the fourth lesson, the teacher presents one of ten sequential science lessons she has designed for third-graders. Many sensory inputs keep her students involved in the lesson as they listen to a "guest scientist." They repeat and act out jingles to aid memory, read about and conduct experiments, analyze and write about results, and categorize their ideas using graphic representations.

Kindergarten Mathematics: Caring and a Challenge

Combine fun and learning and you'll always have success.

When asked how they know their teacher is good, I have found that younger students tend to say that their teacher cares about them. Older students are more likely to emphasize that a good teacher challenges them with difficult work and complex thinking tasks. As a kindergarten teacher at Weaver Elementary School in Los Alamitos, Trisha Callella offered both to her students.

First comes the caring. "Parker!"—she addresses a silent boy in the middle of the pack sitting on the rug. "How's your morning today? Did you eat breakfast? Good! What's wrong?" He whispers an answer to which she responds with an empathetic, "Oh yeah? Okay. Come here, sweetie," as she wraps her arms around him and gives him a squeeze. "Let's take off your jacket 'cause it's nice and toasty in here," she says as the two of them work to roll the parka off his shoulders and tug it loose from his arms. Once he is settled, she begins again.

Next comes the challenge. The kindergarten curriculum standards at the time this lesson was taught called for children to learn to count from 1 to 20. These five- and six-year-olds intently focus for a half-hour on counting up to 100 by ones, twos, fours, fives, and tens. They work alone, quickly counting the numbers on charts in their laps, or together as a class, counting groups of numbers as their teacher flips the answers on a set of 100 blocks strung on rods in rows of ten. They write and calculate equations when Dr. Callella asks if two groups of ten plus seven are 27. Then, they practice organizing numbers into groups of two or ten to make counting more efficient. Toward the end of this practice time, the students demonstrate the commutative property of addition by solving equations such as eight plus (blank) equals (blank) plus eight.

Naming and counting numbers are foundational skills. Understanding what the numbers represent and how to use them to solve problems are next steps up in mathematical thinking. The children are now ready to use that foundation to construct and solve their own word problems. Dr. Callella randomly selects Janet to make up a problem. Janet describes a rabbit eating two carrots and then eating six more. Each child uses a "number line," a strip of paper listing positive and negative numbers from zero to 20 or more, to find out how many carrots the rabbit ate altogether.

Dr. Callella asks the class, "Why does Janet have six carrots and then two more carrots?" A student explains, "Two plus six is the same as six plus two." When the teacher asks "why" again, Amalia elaborates, "If you start with the big number and hop to the little number, then you'll get the same answer." Building on her comment, Dr. Callella shows on a chart in front of the class how putting the larger number first, then adding the smaller number is quicker and more efficient than starting with the smaller number.

An observer sees clearly that even at their young age, her students comprehend the commutative property of addition. They can also understand the advantages of switching the order of numbers because it can be more efficient to count on from a higher number, even if that wasn't the first addend presented to them.

In an interview, Dr. Callella explains the process she used in this demonstration lesson. She points out the components of the math wall she had created and used while teaching. Divided into sections, it matched the six mathematical strands for kindergarten set out in that year's California curriculum standards:

1. Number Sense & Operations
2. Algebraic Reasoning
3. Patterns & Functions
4. Discrete Math; Logical & Deductive Reasoning
5. Spatial Sense, Geometry, Measurement
6. Data Analysis, Statistics, Probability

In her daily lessons, students always do the "warm-up" activities and the first two math strands. The teacher adds other strands to the lesson based on what the children are prepared to handle. By March, when this lesson was presented, the students had mastered every kindergarten standard for the year set by the state and her school district. When the children arrived in Dr. Callella's class in August, only two of them could recognize numbers beyond ten and seven were second-language learners. They were a cluster of very young children coming to Weaver from 9 school districts and 11 cities. She confessed that this group was particularly "fun" and "challenging," and, in fact, she later called this her toughest class in 15 years of teaching. They started with few self-help and problem-solving skills. Some had no preschool experience. Behavior problems kept popping up in class until January. Dr. Callella says her students drive her teaching.

> I'm just following them. Wherever they go is where we'll end up, but we've completed the expectations for what they want us to do in K. The potential is so far advanced, and they can do so much more than the standards reflect or expect. Right now, they're just beginning to understand groups. They're understanding early place values in math. According to our report card, they are finished, but obviously they're not.
>
> I'm a big risk-taker. I follow the kids and if I see they're almost ready for something, I'll try it. Usually, nine times out ten, it's pretty success-ful and then we tweak it along the way. It's a very dynamic process so that the children are continually being challenged at a level that's right for them. They call it the "zone of proximal development"— that's right where they're able to learn. So, it's not too challenging, not too easy, kind of that mama bear stuff. It's just right, so they can con-tinually learn. And, I get that information from calling on children ran-domly rather than calling on kids who are raising their hands. I also get that from looking at kids who are using their boards. They're not just staring at me doing the work. Everything on the math wall they have

in their packet. So, because they are sitting there doing it, I'm able to monitor if I need to help someone. I'm able to see which strategies are out there and share them on that given day. They're learning from each other. The most informative thing for me is that every child is doing everything at every moment. There's 100 percent participation. It's random selection, so I know who is learning, who really is understanding, and what I need to do next.

Some children will be direct modeling, where they need to trade one thing for one thing. Some children will be able to trade ten things for a ten stick. They are able to hold onto a number; there's some number constancy. This approach really follows individual children and challenges each of them at his or her level by providing different tools and different strategies. The children really teach each other.

One thing I found for my class that they needed more of was more re-phrasing rather than hearing the problem once and then doing it. They forget. They're working with carrots. They forget what they're working with. So, by adding the re-phrasing element to the math wall, they're understanding that the focus is on the content of what you're trying to do, not just on grabbing numbers. Part of that process is understanding the problem itself.

I'm trained as a reading specialist in following children. If you tell them what they have to learn, you'll be missing so many children. Yet, if you follow them and provide different opportunities, the children will be able to reach and even exceed those expectations. I am truly passionate about the fact that you have to be willing to change what you're doing in the classroom based on the children. Just because I was able to do certain things last year that worked really, really well for those children, honestly, not a single thing done last year is being done again because these are the polar opposite children in my classroom this year.

One other thing I'd like to say about what I do in the classroom is that I think that everything should be fun. I mean, they are five years old! There needs to be a great deal of movement, a lot of interaction that's keeping them engaged doing things rather than talking at them. Let them participate, give them a great deal of choices, and have high but realistic expectations. They love challenges. Combine fun and learning and you'll always have success.

I think the one message I would love for every teacher to believe is that everything is in the expectations. You have to believe that every single child can learn and deserves to be challenged. Just because the bar is set here [raises her hand waist high] doesn't mean that's all they can achieve. I think sometimes it's easy to underestimate what

children can do based on their background and based on where
they're from. The expectations are simply too low. If they love learning, they will learn and it doesn't matter where they come from. They
all can achieve and go way beyond the kindergarten expectations as
I see now.

Box 1.2   Pause & Reflect

Did anything in this teaching example surprise you? If so, why?

Dr. Callella has had great success with her students. What does she do
with the children in this lesson that may contribute to their success?

First-Grade Writing: Super Sentences and Juicy Words

The humongous snake slithered through the tall green grass.

With a dramatic flair, Maureen Clair mesmerizes five- and six-year-olds by
modulating her voice and bending near to make eye contact. She gently
prods her class of first-graders at Landell Elementary in Cypress to write
"super sentences" using "juicy" words.

"What's another word for big?" she asks.

Students offer, "Huge," "Humongous," "Large," "Gigantic."

Working at the whiteboard, the teacher models writing complex sentences
suggested by the students. She color-codes the noun (blue), the action or verb
(red), the adjective or description (yellow), and adverbs or adverbial phrases
(green). Like magic, she teaches them to substitute their juicy verbs, adjectives,
and adverbs for "boring" words they hear all the time. Then, she shows them
how to rearrange the color-coded words and phrases to make the sentence
livelier. Students are asked to write their own sentences by providing fresh
descriptors and organizing the words in interesting ways. They start off writing simple sentences such as "It is big," and then progress to more complex
lines such as, "The humongous snake slithered through the tall, green grass."
Budding authors are in the making in this first-grade class.

In an interview, Ms. Clair described her approach:

At a young level, it really helped them to write "super sentences" and
learn how to move the sentence structure by underlining things and

color-coding them. The "who" is colored this color and the "when" another. And then they really learned that you can start with the "when" piece. I found out children become much better writers if you start really early in the year with this approach because one of the writing objectives at first grade is that when they do their final writing, they can't have sentences that start with the same word. Little guys write a lot of "the" this and "the" that, and "It did. It did." Early in the year, I started at the beginning by taking little sentences and moving parts. By the end of the year, they know to check themselves. . . . The other thing I tried when I was working on teaching writing with my mentor was that she actually had me put in front of them the rubric that I was going to be scoring them with. I had every child over the 90th percentile on the final writing assessment those two years.

Ms. Clair was then assigned a kindergarten class and she discovered that with rigorous instruction even these younger children can accomplish more than had been expected of them in the past:

I found out that our little kindergartners are ready and have enough phonemic awareness to start writing on their own in January. They write by themselves. We also saw that children had mastered 100 high-frequency words. I found that with those little kindergartners, some would master as many as 800 high-frequency words. I learned to let them go when they are ready. I had two children test out in our Reading Counts program and their Lexile scores were fourth grade in kindergarten.

Box 1.3 Pause & Reflect

How do you think Ms. Clair changed in her teaching over time?

Does her teaching in this example look similar or different from what K-1 teachers you know do? In what ways?

Second-Grade Reading: A Master of Organization

Developing a good set of strategies.

Continuous assessment drives instruction in Evan Grandon's second-grade reading class at Weaver Elementary. Using "Running Records" regularly to identify which students need specific types of teaching, she not only introduces phonics and reading strategies such as "chunking words" to the whole class, but she also divides students up into small reading groups so that she can give more individualized attention within a 20-minute timeframe. For the few who need it, she first attends to basic reading skills. With the more adept readers, her focus is on a broader range of language arts development.

Several times during the year, she reorganizes the groups based on whether individual children have mastered specific skills and are ready to move on to more challenging material. These groups are not static. Currently, she has five groups and meets with four of them on four days of the week. The fifth group is comprised of two students working to expand vocabulary with a larger set of high-frequency words. They meet with her five days each week. Two groups are practicing how to retell a story and thereby develop greater comprehension of the text. Monitoring their own understanding of nonfiction material is the focus of the fourth group. Advanced second-graders, who are reading at the end of third-grade level, engage in a more in-depth conversation about their books. The different teaching approaches she uses illustrate how Ms. Grandon shapes instruction to match students' levels of achievement to further advance their learning.

Skillful organization makes it possible for her to conduct small-group instruction while other students continue productive work on their own. While waiting for the smallest group of students to settle in at the table with Ms. Grandon, I notice that calm, order, and peacefulness reign here. Children throughout the room are quietly reading and working on assignments. Student volunteers from this class are available to assist those who might have questions while the teacher is occupied.

Allison and Jason sit on the outside edge of a U-shaped table, with the instructor sitting within arm's reach inside the U. These two pupils need more work on phonics and vocabulary. Ms. Grandon states the purpose of today's lesson—to practice reading, writing, and spelling "high-frequency" words they often see and hear. She teaches them to recognize a "sight word" such as "how" and use what they know about that word—the "ow" sound—to decipher other words with that same sound. On small whiteboards, her two charges practice writing and correctly spelling the sight words. Ms. Grandon shows them how to "chunk" sounds within words and then put them together as in the word "air . . . craft." Reading with fluency and good phrasing comes next. The children read two- and three-word phrases from the card stock Ms. Grandon flips up for a quick view.

The lesson concludes with each child softly reading aloud from his or her own copy of the same book. Many of the words and sounds they reviewed earlier appear again in this text. Ms. Grandon takes notes on the errors each child makes, when each self-corrects an error, and strategies each employs to decode the text. She will use these notes to plan instruction for tomorrow that will match the skills the children still need. Assigned homework involves reading the story again, this time with expression, and delving into the meaning of the story by finding the part where the main character is surprised and determining why that is. Ms. Grandon's short but thorough lesson incorporates phonics, vocabulary, fluency, and interpretation of the text at the "just right" level for these two youngsters.

The next group of six children are reading a nonfiction book about sharks' senses. They are working on expanding their vocabularies using a strategy called "exclusion brainstorming" that calls for them to predict which words will and will not appear in the book. From a dozen or so words on paper in front of them, each child circles the words that he or she expects to see while reading and then explains the rationale for each choice. When explaining their reasoning, the students refer to what they have learned before about sharks and they articulate the logic behind their selections. The children move on to read the book using soft voices. When the teacher taps the eraser on her pencil in front of one of them, that student reads slightly louder so the teacher can hear and take notes. Ms. Grandon coaches a student on how to chunk words to figure them out or re-read and use clues from the text about the meaning of the word. She helps students decipher vocabulary words, corrects errors in pronunciation, or has the children present counter-arguments when one student's reasoning is weak. Homework for these students is to write a question about the book that will be a "stumper" for the others to answer when they meet the next day.

After the lesson, Ms. Grandon explains:

My goal is for these guys to leave as balanced readers. One thing I try to develop in them is to have a good set of strategies. In the first group, the students both came to me needing a lot of work with high-frequency word usage and spelling. I've been working on the eraser game. We typically do that for two or three days out of the week to build their high-frequency word knowledge—knowing how to use the words, how to read the words, how to spell the words. I always introduce the lesson with some kind of high-frequency word. I went into chunking because that is something I noticed through assessment that the kids are not able to do, and a lot of their mistakes were through phonics. So rather than just teaching them phonics skills, which we do whole class, I think it's more appropriate and beneficial to have it taught through a strategy so they can apply that strategy to any text. They could use chunking in the text today that had the "ai" making the long "a" sound, but they could also use that chunking strategy any other time that they need to chunk. They learn the strategy, but they're working on the phonics skills. I see a hole or a flaw in their fluency—in their phrasing—so I show them those phrasing cards. I lift those up quickly. It trains their eyes to see two words at a time first, and then we move on to three words at a time. Then, I had them read their text. We do more comprehension follow-up work the following day.

With the second group, all those kids have great decoding strategies already. They know what to do when they get stuck on a word. At times, they need reminders of what to do, but their goal for me—because they have all of the pieces of decoding, they have good fluency, and they have pretty decent retell and comprehension—is to expand their vocabulary. That is why every day when we do exclusion brainstorming, we learn about 9 to 12 new words. A third of the words are words that will be in the text that I want them to know. A third of the words they could expect to be in the text, but will not be in there. The last third of the words, they don't expect to be in the text but will be. They really have to use their predicting strategy to decipher which words will be in there and which words will not be in there. The last big piece you saw today is the monitoring of comprehension, which is the trickiest part for these guys as they read nonfiction. We find out through research that when kids have a good understanding of nonfiction, whenever they go to read a story about sharks, now that they have all of that background knowledge about sharks, they'll be able to have a deeper understanding of the text. We've taken a turn from moving from different pieces of comprehension to more specific development of nonfiction comprehension skills.

Box 1.4   Pause & Reflect

What are the strengths of this lesson? How do the students benefit from the instruction?

Third-Grade Science with "Guests"

Einstein's ideas of gravity waves ... They can understand a concept like that!

On a regular basis, Lisa McClellan "performs" when she teaches science to third-graders at McGaugh Elementary School in Los Alamitos, but it isn't the drama or the occasional silliness that make her excellent at her job, though these attributes certainly help. It is the detailed planning of her science units and the thoughtfulness behind the construction of each lesson that make her teaching so powerful.

Throughout the year, each new topic is introduced by a "scientist" whose personality reflects his or her discovery and serves as a mnemonic device to help students remember the ideas. Based, in part, on Stephen Hawking's television series on the history of our understanding of the universe, ten scientists "visit" the classroom to talk about a particular breakthrough each made in comprehending our world. The discoveries start at a simple level and are used as steppingstones to the next stories which are about more abstract concepts. The topics are tied to what were at that time the somewhat loosely written third-grade state science standards. Students were expected to become familiar with the periodic table and learn information such as: "the sun is a source of energy;" "nuclear fusion makes energy and elements are formed during that process;" and "gravity is a primary force in the behavior of the universe."

Today's lesson is a study of light. Ms. McClellan, wearing a lab coat and speaking with a German accent, shows up in class as Joseph von Fraunhofer, the inventor of the spectroscope. Von Fraunhofer describes how he discovered black lines in light coming from the sun when he viewed it through his newly made telescope lens. He wonders whether the colors and lines he sees could be indicators of elements and chemicals that make up the sun. Two classes of students in the room together discuss with "the scientist" how elements may absorb and emit different colors depending on their structure. To explore this concept, the students use spectroscopes they themselves have made to examine a variety of light sources—candle light, hydrogen, phosphorous, helium, neon, mercury—and record the color and pattern of lines each produces. They now have a way to identify elements they have seen on a periodic chart.

When asked about what works for her in teaching science, Ms. McClellan mentions specific techniques she uses. She includes kinesthetic and mnemonic devices associated with abstract concepts to help the students remember. One example is using a "hand jive" or a motto in association with a concept such as gravity or inertia. She demonstrates by putting her hands together like a pillow under her tilted head and chanting, "An object at rest, stays at rest." Twirling her hands around each other, she declares, "An object in motion stays in motion . . . unless there's friction," as she brushes her hands together . . . swish, swish. To teach abstract ideas, she provides experiences that demonstrate the concept. Students see the spectrum of light. They do something physical. They don't just hear and read about it.

Role-playing the part of a scientist adds humor and helps maintain the attention of her class. More important, the storytelling illustrates the significance of the scientific concept, which greatly improves the odds that her pupils will remember what they have witnessed.

The teacher uses icons developed by Sandra Kaplan at the University of Southern California to label the various types of thinking students exhibit, to expand upon one or more of them, and to add to the complexity of thinking involved in a task. As students talk about ideas presented by the scientist at the start of the lesson, or ask questions during the discussion, the second teacher in the room writes notes summarizing each statement and attaches an icon next to the comment. It may be a picture of lips representing "language of the discipline" being used, or petals on a flower showing "details" that are added, or a Greek temple to stand for a "big idea."

Creating relevant participatory activities for her third-graders is one of Ms. McClellan's most successful teaching strategies. The lesson above involved looking at lamps to see the spectrum of light from different sources and identifying the lines on the spectrum showing the elements. Then the students compared what they found with charts of different elements and the light patterns they produce. They finished by drawing what they observed. The lesson was all about engaging the students in doing the work of scientists and making their own discoveries.

"Students are excited and interested in how things work. It is the 'Why is the sky blue?' question. They get a sense of power when they formulate some conjectures and explain them to someone else. They become self-motivated learners," explained Ms. McClellan.

The debriefing toward the end of the lesson allows students to talk about what discoveries they made and permits the teacher to summarize pertinent information. When there are discrepancies between students' findings and their conjectures, they often generate other ideas about ways to get answers to their questions. During these discussions, students describe in their own words the evidence they collected and the conclusions they have drawn, which helps to cement that knowledge. What they learned and the questions they still have are recognized as a significant part of the lesson.

Learning is measured in a variety of ways. One part of this instructor's final exam asks students to teach a lesson to their parents and then test their parents' understanding of the scientific concepts presented. If the students can effectively teach the information, it strongly indicates they have gained a deeper comprehension of the subject than a traditional test might reveal.

In a later interview, Ms. McClellan shares more of her thoughts on teaching science at an elementary school level.

I think that kids need multiple exposures to concepts. They need a lot of "hands on." Looking at literature, this means discussing a lot of literature. If it's writing, they need to be doing a lot of writing. And if it is science, they need to be doing a lot of experiments and doing them often, not just once. Doing them for other people. Doing them wrong, correcting it, and finding out why. Doing related things. Coming up with their own experiments. So, lots of hands-on activity. Also, I gradually increase the difficulty of the concepts. I don't hesitate to start off the beginning of our unit on gravity waves with Einstein's ideas of gravity waves. They can understand a concept like that. It's almost as though they don't have any predetermined barriers against science or against math, or a belief that only certain people can do that. They're open to those ideas. So, you can go for something exciting and big as long as you break it down, kind of starting backwards to plan how to get to that big idea. They like complexity. They like it to be important. They like the idea that perhaps somebody else doesn't know it. Perhaps their moms or dads don't know that. They like the challenge of the discovery. They like to know that the information is going to be useful. So, it's really important to contextualize it and show them how either this is something that is happening on an everyday basis for them, or it's going to help them understand larger phenomena, larger systems, and larger patterns in life or in nature. It is like that kind of back and forth, connecting it to the world and connecting it to them. This is important because it helps them understand what's important about the universe and their place in it.

Box 1.5   Pause & Reflect

What is one important idea you might take away from Ms. McClellan's lesson and interview?

Excellent Teaching and Remarkable Learners

The best educators show us that gifted instruction is both an intellectual and an emotional enterprise. It requires specialized skills rarely seen even in smart and eager novices. Superb teaching demonstrates a day-to-day and week-to-week preparedness to create learning experiences geared to every child in the classroom. It takes time to develop and master the complexities of organizing classrooms, comprehending and sequencing substantive content, planning instruction, and managing the social dynamics of children's interactions. Great teachers listen carefully to children to understand how they are grasping the subject matter, and with experience they can predict typical misconceptions students will have. Those teachers are then able to build upon and re-shape students' thinking. The very best teachers are designers, problem-solvers, and evaluators.

Many of us perceive good students as passive recipients of information. Poor students too frequently are viewed as reluctant participants or resisters. Masterful teachers can transform both high- and low-performing students into more involved, productive, and independent tool users. Inspired students will approach their schoolwork as active scholars, not passive recipients. As members of the school community, they will be far more likely to contribute to the learning of others as they work diligently on improving their own schoolwork. Children taught by excellent instructors become capable achievers, ever-growing in their skills and knowledge, playing a more active and responsible role in advancing their own learning. These are the kinds of results we want for every child. To move toward achieving outcomes such as these, most teachers first need to be exposed to inspiring exemplars of great teaching. After such encounters, many begin to set much higher expectations for what their students will be able to accomplish and what they themselves can succeed in teaching to them.

Summary

The first step to great teaching is to acknowledge the fact that both teachers and students can achieve higher levels than we previously deemed possible.

For too long, all of us—administrators, teachers, parents, policymakers—have settled for adequate performances rather than aiming for excellence. We need to raise our expectations for what can be accomplished in teaching and learning. Watching great teachers inspires others to raise their sights on what they believe they can achieve. An observation tool, such as the lenses presented earlier in this chapter, may help educators as well as other observers focus on components of gifted teaching and notice the complexities within each aspect. Examples of rigorous instruction illuminate how much more can be accomplished by superior teachers.

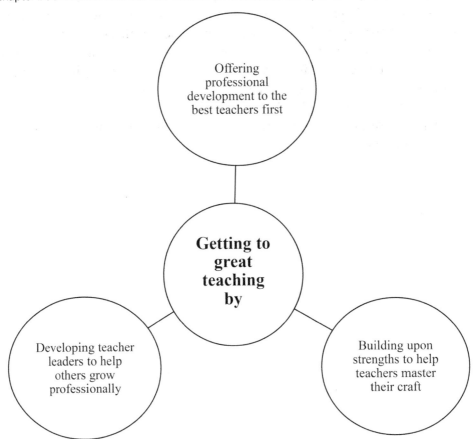

2

Invest in the Best and Build upon Strengths

This chapter addresses three important topics: Choosing the Best; Building upon Strengths; and Growing Teacher Leadership. These three steps work together to help teachers and schools achieve the goal of getting to great teaching. To achieve that result, school and district leaders need to rely on the most highly skilled and motivated teachers at their schools to step up to perfect their instruction by augmenting their repertoires of teaching strategies and, in some cases, completely altering their approaches. Administrators need to invest first in the best teachers by allocating resources to improve their teaching, providing individualized training which builds upon those teachers' strengths, selecting exemplary educators as mentors and coaches to help these individuals practice new approaches in their classrooms, and offer feedback.

Investing in the development of the best teachers first may seem counterintuitive, but it is an approach which works to advance the quality of teaching at a school. These experienced and respected teachers, who have devoted themselves to polishing their craft, can help establish new and higher expectations for what quality instruction looks like and lay the foundation for more improvement among the rest of the faculty.

Schools and districts are correctly concerned about solving problems. They need to counsel out of the profession those teachers who are poor performers, or assist them in becoming competent. Unfortunately, little attention is given to the rest of the improvement equation—how to help the adequate, competent, or even the exceptionally good teachers become even more highly skilled. Rather than focusing solely on boosting the quality of schooling by pushing the least well equipped up from the bottom to improve, more can be accomplished by pulling the entire school up to the top using the best teachers as models, trainers, and standard-bearers for superb teaching.

Starting with the best teachers is a unique approach for improving instruction and getting better results for kids. It works particularly well when professional development is designed to focus on the strengths of each participant. This is different from the common practice of providing all teachers with the same training regardless of their prior experience or expertise in the subject. The cultural tradition of schools is to strive for uniformity and offer equal opportunities by giving the same training to all educators. As a result, many teachers sit through workshops they do not need, while others gain new skills. By centering professional development on the strengths of individual teachers, the movement toward greatness in teaching becomes a realizable goal. Personalizing professional development plans means that instructors can focus on their strengths in teaching and push toward perfecting their skills. Each person can refine his or her teaching techniques based upon what each is ready to learn.

Choosing the Best

Principals may have a difficult time selecting the best teachers for specialized professional development. They are put in an awkward position when they alone must determine the "best" teachers at their schools for the privilege of getting even better. It is especially trying when resources are limited and principals can choose only a few teachers from a faculty of many competent instructors eager to improve their techniques even more. A better approach would be to let other knowledgeable and unbiased individuals make the selection for the principal.

Inviting every certified teacher at a school to apply for the first round of comprehensive professional development is the first step in a fair and open process of selection. Applicants may request that they be the beneficiary of the training, be a mentor to others, or be selected for either position. The next step is to form a small selection team of three or four accomplished teachers and administrators from other schools or districts. Teachers should make up half or more of the team. This team observes each person teach a complete lesson of his or her choice in a content area of the individual's strength. Then, they interview the applicants to learn more about them and to try to determine which candidates are most likely to benefit from the training, and potentially reach superior levels of teaching in the time available. The team recommends one exceptionally skilled instructor who might serve as a mentor to the others. At the same time, the team should identify up to eight teachers they recommend for the learning opportunity in the first round. With the principal's approval, the team notifies individuals about whether they were or were not chosen to participate.

What do selection team members look for when they choose the best candidates for the professional development program and a full-time mentor position? Competent teachers use diverse approaches. Very good teaching can take many shapes and forms. Each person on the team may have his or her own vision of good instruction to offer, but each also benefits from keeping an open mind and considering others' points of view. Any team wants to see students engaged with challenging content. They want to observe a clear and coherent lesson with all the parts from start to finish tied together into a logical whole. Every member would like to find students who can articulate what they are doing in their class assignments, as well as explain why they are doing it. Each might be pleased to see the instructor model how to approach a task or to find students modeling for the class. But using a checklist of specific teaching behaviors may not be particularly useful. One teacher may state the objective of the day's task at the start, while another may make that same objective clear while summarizing conclusions drawn out at the end of the lesson. Students learn more from some assignments by trying out their own procedures rather than following the exact steps demonstrated by the teacher. A reasonable approach to identifying the best teachers is to watch the students to see how they comprehend the instruction and if they have added to their knowledge or skill as a result. Try to assess or determine if the students were stretched in their thinking as they worked. Consider whether the goals and tasks made sense, and whether the assignment was worth doing. Listen to the students' conversation. Was it on task and were they engaged in the work? Who did most of the talking and most of the work? In discussion with other team members, listen carefully to what they observed that showed them good teaching was taking place. Interviews can help team members understand why a teacher chose one method of instruction over another, what he intended to accomplish with individual children, or how he sees himself benefiting if selected for the program.

Choosing the best person to be the mentor is equally difficult. Teams want a high-quality and well-respected instructor for this role. They also will be seeking a good facilitator for adult learning, rather than someone anxious to direct others by telling them how to teach. Interviews with mentor candidates may help the team know more about the assets and expertise of each person so that they can find a mentor who would work well with the teachers selected to participate.

Making good choices among the candidates results in the very best teachers at the school becoming the pioneers trying out a comprehensive professional learning experience. These individuals are the ones likely to become excellent because of their professional study. They are also likely to be people who can lead and interest other faculty members in these professional development options. They will be the ones to assist as demonstration teachers and coaches for others.

Building upon Strengths

Starting with a strength may be a surprising idea to many educators. Accomplished teachers typically are their own harshest critics. Because their aims are high, they are the first to say how they have failed to reach their goals and often want to tackle areas of their greatest weaknesses first. Choosing this direction, however, is not the most advantageous way to travel the road toward great teaching.

It is a bit like tackling Mount Everest. It is best to be a very good hiker before you take on the challenge. If you want to reach the pinnacle, isn't it prudent to start at a base camp part way up? The distance to the top is shorter and the potential for achieving the goal is significantly greater. Having attained confidence and new skills in teaching one subject puts teachers in a better position to strive later for improvement in weaker areas where their foundations are less secure. Skills learned in an area of strength are often useful in improving other aspects of teaching as well.

John Gerbrandt, from San Lorenzo Elementary in Felton, taught for more than 30 years before he applied for a two-year fellowship with the Art of Teaching. John explains how he treasured the opportunity to improve upon his strength during professional development.

I got to choose the subject area I wanted to excel in. For all those years, it had been ingrained in me to work on the areas I most needed to improve or a subject which wasn't quite as exciting to me as other curriculum subjects. So, when our six fellows first met, we all decided to concentrate on reading and writing. I've enjoyed teaching language arts over the years and I felt that I had become a good teacher in this area, so I agreed to work on language arts. The next week in meeting with my mentor, she asked me if language arts was a passion of mine. I told her I enjoyed it, but she again asked me if it was a passion of mine. I honestly told her "no" and that teaching mathematics was what I really enjoyed the most. That was my teaching passion.

This led me to my second "ah ha!" moment. This program is geared for experienced teachers, not just new teachers, and it is to help you delve into your teaching passion and take it to the next level. So, I decided to switch from the rest of the group and pursue a deeper level of teaching in the area of math for my fifth-grade students. . . . I've always felt that I had been a good math teacher. I have for many years embraced teaching math first on a concrete level using manipulative materials, then moving to a representation level using symbolic models, and finally to the abstract level. But I knew that I would be learning some new techniques and I was very inspired.

Administrators too have seen the benefits of building on strengths. The principal of Billy Mitchell Elementary in Lawndale, Lucia Laguarda, had a lot to say about the advantages of building on teachers' strongest practices during an online seminar hosted by the National Council of Teachers of English:

Starting with success is a great way to get teacher buy-in. Teachers will listen and learn from each other, especially if there is success, which is contagious. Find out what your good teachers are doing and share that. At Mitchell, we focused on Writer's Workshop because there were enough teachers that had successfully implemented it and were getting great results. Those using Writer's Workshop had taught their students to write as a writer for an audience of readers. Students thought about their own stories and grew them with detail and voice into published pieces that they were proud to share. Students were scoring above the district rubric. The language that teachers had their students use about thinking and writing as a writer, and reading as a reader, transformed all other parts of the day as students grew as learners and thinkers.

Begin to build on strengths by asking teachers to pick a subject for which each has a passion—one each loves to teach and feels confident about getting every student to learn well. Then, teachers can use that passion for the content to motivate students' interest and curiosity.

Teaching has been described as a triangle comprised of three significant components: the teacher, the student, and the subject. All three elements are crucial for learning, including the connection of teacher with the student, as well as the relationship both establish with the content presented. Sharing a personal passion for reading or writing or science with the children is more likely to heighten their interest in the subject as well. Demonstrating you care about how each student understands and thinks about the material can motivate the child to open up about his or her way of thinking as well as questions he or she has about the subject.

Next, teachers can expand their repertoire of strategies for engaging students in learning the content being taught. They strive to get every child in their classes so interested in the subject and so confident of their abilities that all learn significantly more about the subject and improve their skills in using that content. Teachers increase their pedagogical toolkit by getting ideas from others, by reading professional books and current research on teaching and learning, by practicing new techniques while getting feedback from a colleague, and by assessing the effects of new methods on their students so that they can refine how and what they teach. It takes courage to tackle new content and approaches, especially when you are teaching a subject with which you have had success in the past. Doing something new often proves difficult at first, and seems awkward when you were smooth in your delivery before. But having several methods at your disposal inevitably puts you in a position of being better able to find the appropriate approaches for the children before you.

Growing Teacher Leadership

By investing in teachers who are often highly respected by faculty and parents for their successes, skills, and accomplishments, schools develop a wider pool of talented educators who eventually will be well equipped to coach, lead, and share quality teaching practices with others. Some schools and districts already use their strongest teachers to good effect in their efforts to build the capacity of personnel throughout the schools. Round Rock Independent School District in Texas is a good example. They often ask practicing teachers to lead or co-lead professional development at the school and district level. One example is their Reading Rocks program—an initiative to take Reader's Workshop to the next level. At the outset of the program, they asked their elementary school instructors to apply for a one-year course as pilot participants who would then be prepared to be teacher leaders of the Reading Rocks course and other professional development. A teacher at Live Oak Elementary and a winner of the Presidential Award for Excellence in Math and Science Teaching, Erika Hassay, was among those selected. She and the other teacher leaders completed the training, practicing new techniques themselves, and then worked with peers the following year in summer and after-school sessions to share the content of the course and their own experiences with students in the classroom. As Erika pointed out, "Hearing about what works from someone who is in the classroom is well received."

Tustin Unified School District recruited Art of Teaching mentors on their staffs to be coaches when the school system introduced new technology and software districtwide. District leaders wanted teacher leaders who knew the curriculum content and how to teach it very well to be those coaches. These recruits could be trained in how to operate and access the technology, and then they could use their content expertise to show other teachers in the district how to apply these resources to make their teaching stronger. In a nearby town, Los Alamitos Unified asked one of its most successful elementary school teachers, who had completed a fellowship with the Art of Teaching, to coach middle-school educators in how to teach mathematics. She had a solid understanding of the content and sophisticated pedagogical approaches which the district wanted its secondary school teachers to consider using to improve their results.

By investing in the best teachers first, with quality professional development, and building initially on their strong content areas, schools and districts can achieve a level of great teaching faster with the largest number of teachers. Then, the school will have an even larger team of talented instructors who can share their new skills and successes with students by assisting with the school and district professional development.

Summary

Attaining a higher quality level in the teaching of one subject with a year or two of professional development is most likely to be accomplished by teachers who already are good at their jobs and have solid foundations upon which to build. When aiming for greatness is the goal, it is more efficient for principals and superintendents to invest their professional development dollars first in a comprehensive program for the best teachers at each school.

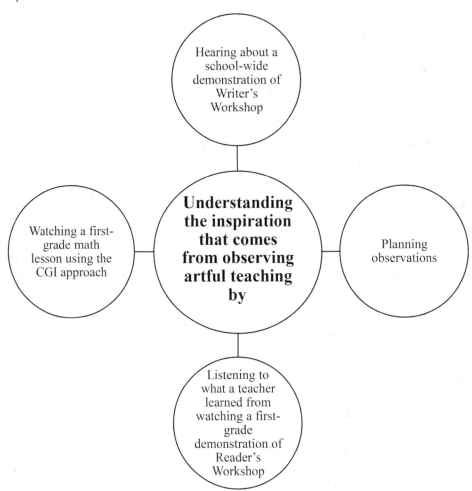

3

Get a Vision: The Power of Observations

Few people know in advance exactly how they want to proceed to improve their teaching. What people need is a vision of what might be possible. They require an introduction to practices that have already been tested with children and found to be of value. These teachers want to see these practices at work in classrooms and observe how children respond to different teaching approaches and difficult content. Once they have been introduced to new methods and experienced the power these approaches have to improve student learning, teachers begin to envision how they can alter and augment their own instruction to be more successful.

"I didn't know what I didn't know!" is a frequent comment from teachers who are able to observe other artful instructors. One group of visitors was particularly startled as they watched a highly accomplished educator successfully ask kindergarten children to create their own math word problems and then use more than one way to solve them. They were surprised by what students understood about text when they watched another skilled professional ask first-graders thoughtful questions about the meaning and theme of a story they had read, pushing thinking to levels the guests had never imagined.

"I want to be able to do that with my kids," exclaimed one of these eager observers.

Through visits like these, teachers begin to embrace a vision of the kind of teaching each of them would like to achieve. The following examples show the types of practices elementary school teachers in Southern

California have observed and suggest how those classroom visits helped shape their views of what makes for great teaching. Substantive curriculum, rigorous assignments, persistence of the children in completing and revising their work, children helping each other learn, differentiation during instruction so that students at a range of skill levels can add to their knowledge and keep advancing in their learning—these are some of the elements of great teaching that inspire visitors. In almost every case, they see pupils tackling tasks normally given to children far above their grade level. Students are tackling assignments which require complex thinking and analytic skills. The independence of the students as they work also impresses many observers. Children are generally enthusiastic, active, and thoroughly engaged in learning. They enjoy the challenges presented to them. These aspects of high-quality teaching and remarkable results are what observers want to achieve themselves. Before looking at three examples of demonstration lessons, consider the preparations that need to be done in advance.

Preparing for Observations

Observations should be focused on one subject. Visiting teachers need to choose the content and grade levels they most want to see being taught. It is possible that when getting started, the school or district can only offer observations for one subject. Over time, however, demonstration classes can be set up for more subjects, and teachers will have more choice. Once the content and levels are determined, someone needs to identify those extraordinary teachers within or outside of the school system who use highly effective methods from which others can learn. Because the goal is for observers to get a bigger vision of what students can learn and do, only the most effective instructors should be included. All potential candidates should be observed by a selection team before they are finally chosen to conduct the demonstration lessons.

The cost of observations is the cost of time and of substitutes to take over the classes of the visiting teachers as well as a substitute for the demonstration teacher during a debriefing session after the lesson. When planning the observation schedule, at least a half-day of release time is needed for each teacher. The visitors will want to see a lesson from start to finish, and then they will want to meet with the demonstration teacher to ask questions about the teaching techniques used and about the effects of this kind of instruction on the children over time. If possible, it is good to have someone facilitate the debriefing session to make sure that the discussion delves deeply into the decisions the demonstration teacher made in both planning and conducting the lesson. The facilitator can help the visitors understand more about how the teacher went about learning the teaching method and how long it has taken him or her to master the practice.

Demonstration teachers usually find these observation days as beneficial as those who attend their lessons. Often, the hosting instructor experiences the dialogue with the visitors during the debriefing sessions as stimulating and reinforcing. It is a rare opportunity to talk about your approach to teaching and how you have seen your students blossom. At the same time, demonstration teachers frequently see their students become even more attentive and articulate about what they are learning when they have an audience.

Groups of teachers from the same school should attend the demonstration lesson. This gives the visitors a chance to discuss what they have seen and learned as they travel home from their observation and when they return to their school. Those teachers who choose to learn more about the practice they observed are likely then to have a partner or a team of colleagues who will join them as they study this new teaching approach.

Surprisingly, large numbers of visitors can observe without disrupting the lesson or disturbing the students' focus on their teacher. A class can easily handle ten spectators, and it is not unusual to have as many as 20 to 25 people in a room at once. The keys to success are preparing in advance and establishing a code of conduct or etiquette for visitations. The demonstration teacher should let students know before the lesson that visitors will be in the room and their purpose is to see how the teacher conducts the lesson. She should explain that the students are to go about their work as usual. If she wants the visitors to interact with students and ask them questions as they work, she should tell the children and the visitors that this may occur. The etiquette for visitors usually includes turning off cell phones and observing quietly during instruction. Guests should not wander about the room looking at work on the walls or taking photos until after the lesson. If the demonstration teacher agrees, visitors may ask the students questions about what they are doing as they work independently or in groups, but they should not step in to coach them unless given permission to do so. Most observers take notes to keep track of the lesson sequence, teaching points, teacher's directions, and the students' responses. During the debriefing session, observers can use their notes to refer to specific parts of the lesson and the behavior of an individual student to explore the demonstration teacher's thinking. What follows are examples of classroom observations and how visiting teachers were inspired by these experiences to learn a new approach to instruction.

School-Wide Writing

Observation days are magical.

Amanda Johnson from Loma Vista Elementary School in Tustin observed writing instruction in several classrooms at Billy Mitchell Elementary in Lawndale. She was aware as she watched that the thinking students were doing about the skill of writing was far more demanding than in the situations more familiar to her. The impression these lessons made on her illustrates the dramatic effect watching exemplary teachers can have on observers' expectations for themselves and their colleagues. Amanda Johnson describes her visit in a short essay:

> Kindergarten writers diligently worked to create fact pages for their "All About Books," while fifth-grade writers analyzed paragraph structure for their fantasy pieces. Students across classrooms and grade levels engaged in the writing process and worked at various levels of development.
>
> During the kindergarten mini-lesson, the teacher, Ruth Gillespie, asked for a "turn-and-talk." The resulting conversations were extremely powerful. Students turned to their partners and immediately began discussing their topics and facts. Though young, these students transformed themselves into writers and held focused conversations.
>
> In the third-grade classroom of Angela Bae and fifth-grade classroom of Liz Adams, students had multiple opportunities to think, discuss, and share their ideas as writers. They were comfortable when asked to share, and understood the expectations for participation.
>
> The post-observation discussion further solidified the evidence that teachers at Billy Mitchell set high expectations for student learning and believe in the power of collaboration. Teachers shared their strategies for planning units along with their yearly timelines. The level of professionalism and teamwork across grade levels was impressive, and it became clear that preparation existed as a joint effort in formulating year-long curricular plans.
>
> Walking away from Billy Mitchell, my mind raced as I considered all the possibilities for not only my own writing classroom, but for our entire school. Observation days are magical, as they allow you to see so many wonderful ways of teaching and learning. Billy Mitchell was indeed one of those magical days, and I was grateful for the experience.

Ms. Johnson took away many lessons from this day, including the sense that higher expectations can and should be set for students; increased student talk about the subject matter is valuable for enhancing student learning; and students can be taught to have focused conversations in which they share their understandings with each other.

Box 3.1   Pause & Reflect

Amanda Johnson wanted to share her observations with other teachers. What did she describe that struck you as important? What questions did you have about the lessons that Amanda observed?

Do teachers in your school or district observe each other? If so, do you discuss what you saw and ask questions of each other?

First-Grade Reading

In walked the love of reading.

When Cathy Lien, a teacher at Heideman Elementary in Tustin, saw a videotaped lesson taught by Jodi Manby at Billy Mitchell, she was impressed. After all, Ms. Manby's lesson with her first-graders involved using metacognition, the process of thinking about one's own thinking to better comprehend a text, and making deep and personal connections to better understand the characters in a story. Teaching students to think about their own thinking processes and analyzing reading material in this way was new for Ms. Lien.

The lesson structure was also unfamiliar to her. It included two brief mini-lessons during which the teacher modeled these reading strategies, independent reading time for children to read books they selected, and individual conferences during which the teacher complimented each child on a strength in reading and taught a new skill to those who were ready. Ms. Lien saw in this lesson ways she could organize and manage to teach children in her own classroom who were at different levels of skill. She could see the value of and method for differentiating instruction based on the needs of individual children.

Many of these children spoke Spanish at home, so any opportunities to speak were important for their English-language development. In Ms. Manby's classroom, they were given lots of time to talk with each other about their reading and to practice using their metacognitive "thinking stems" or "sentence starters." Sentences and phrases such as "What makes you say that?" "Tell me more," and "I'm thinking that . . ." are written on the board for the children to use with their partners. Teaching students ways to have respectful conversations, while presenting their points of view with evidence to back them up, is a sign of great teaching going on in this class.

In the video, Ms. Manby injects energy into the lesson by walking around the edge of the carpet, wading into various groups, moving closer to individual children, and reading with expression. She also has a way of making her lessons conversational and personal. After giving directions to the children, she will say "Capisci?" and the students answer with "Capisci" to show they understand.

"I have a book for you," she says, and then continues in a whisper as she leans toward them and shares her secret. "By Angela Johnson. *One of Three*."

She holds the book up, showing them the cover illustration, and asks what they are thinking, wondering, noticing, and even visualizing. She tells them to talk with partners about the thoughts that come to mind about this new book, *One of Three*. After reading the first sentence to the class, Ms. Manby explains that it is about sisters and one of them is called Nicky.

"I know a lot about sisters!" she exclaims. "I have three and one called Nicky." The class gasps. Continuing to draw the children in by sharing relevant tidbits from her own life and dramatizing parts of the story, she reads to them with frequent breaks for them to talk about the connections to this story that they are discovering for themselves. This demonstration teacher shares her personal interests and stories, connecting that to the content and enticing the children into the reading material at the same time.

The children then move into private nooks, sitting at tables or lying on the rug, as they read books of their choice. Ms. Manby engages in individual conversations with child after child, pulling up a chair or stretching out on the rug to get at eye level.

"You did something impressive as a reader," she says. "You were speaking your thoughts out loud."

She models how to read with expression for one student and then asks, "Do I kind of sound like a mother frog?"

"Let me see," she ponders with another child. "You told me what you notice. You told me why you thought that. You told me your evidence. Wow! You are doing real reading."

Following independent reading, the teacher calls the children together for a lesson on the difference between surface connections and deep or meaningful connections. Using *Wemberly Worried* as the text, she points out that "Wemberly has a purple dress and I have a purple dress. Does my connection to her dress help me understand what is happening with her?"

"No!" the class shouts.

"It's a surface connection. Not a meaningful connection," she says.

Together they examine more meaningful connections that do help them understand the character more deeply.

After watching Ms. Manby's video, Ms. Lien attended a training led by this gifted teacher, seeing in person how she teaches utilizing the methods called Reader's Workshop and Writer's Workshop. She describes how that experience totally transformed her teaching:

> I teach a combo class of amazing first- and second-graders. Flashback to three years ago. I had been teaching a one–two combo for a couple of years. It looked something like this: Give the second-graders something to do while I teach the first-graders. Then give the first-graders something to do while I teach the second-graders. This process would go on all day long for reading, writing, and math. Wash. Rinse. Repeat. Exhausting, yes. Artful? Not so much.
>
> Enter my first workshop training. It happened to be in Writer's Workshop. Since my site had chosen it as our signature practice, I would be learning both workshop models [reading and writing] at the same time. Yay, me! Into the classroom I strolled, both eager and apprehensive at the same time, and who do I see leading the training? Jodi Manby—*the* Jodi Manby.
>
> "Isn't she the teacher I saw in a video demonstrating artful teaching?" I wondered to myself. "Jackpot!!"
>
> Before she could start her presentation, I approached her with this question, "How am I supposed to teach Reader's and Writer's Workshop twice a day and still fit in all other content areas as well?"
>
> She smiled and calmly replied, "Workshop is a combo teacher's dream."
>
> By the end of the day, I understood. Over the next two years this exhausted combo teacher transformed into an inspired teacher. Gone were the days of reading out of two different anthologies and teaching to only half the room at a time. In walked embedded differentiation through mini-lessons, independent reading, effective partner reading, strategy groups, and conferring. In walked six- and seven-year-old students who had the stamina to read for 40 minutes at a time.

In walked a group of students reading at their own level in texts they had chosen themselves. In walked a community of learners who were avid readers—readers who skillfully discussed books with each other in a manner I had never seen before. In walked the love of reading.

Ms. Lien culled from her observations the signs of excellence she then wanted to emulate. She wanted to raise her expectations for what students could achieve, differentiate instruction within a single lesson to pinpoint the needed skills of each child, and engage the children in the material to be learned, using her exuberance for the subject and her personal connections to the material.

Box 3.2   Pause & Reflect

If you had watched the video of Ms. Manby, what one thing impressed you about her teaching? What questions would you have wanted to ask her in a follow-up meeting?

First-Grade Mathematics

It is the ability of the children to articulate their thinking and the methods they use.

As visitors observed Teri Malpass at Weaver Elementary in Los Alamitos, the first thing they noticed was that this teacher makes extraordinarily good use of time for herself and her pupils. Not a moment is wasted. A math lesson begins with 30 minutes of whole-class practice, using the math wall she has designed. The wall is composed of plastic, erasable sheets which are labeled and arranged in sections on one side of the classroom. First-graders sit on the rug facing the wall, which has been set up to help them solve a range of problems for that day. Students come up front to write answers to questions posed by the teacher.

The sequence of the lesson moves through activities that involve the calendar, tally marks, money, a game of elimination from a hundreds chart, fact families, time, the weather report, fractions, and doubling. Forty-five minutes working on a word problem follows the math wall practice. The state math standards covered throughout the lesson range from first through third grade.

The problem to be solved today is:

Tyler gave his mom ___ pieces of candy for Mothers' Day. Three out of four pieces of candy had nuts. How many pieces of candy had nuts? How many pieces of candy didn't have nuts?

Below the problem are three number sets including:

$(3 \times 25 + 3 \times 3)$ $(8 + 8)$ $(18 \times 25 + 102)$

Each child chooses one set of numbers, computes the answer, and uses it to fill in the blank in the word problem. Then, the child goes on to answer the two questions posed in the problem by illustrating the steps used to find a solution and writing the equations with the answers. Most notable is seeing how much choice students have when approaching the same problem. They choose the numbers they will use within the problem and that establishes the level of challenge for them. They choose the tools they will use to solve the problem and the strategies they will employ to find answers.

Students read the problem silently and then one child reads it aloud to the class. Together they review the parts of the problem to make certain they know what it is about and what they are trying to solve. Then, they set to work while Ms. Malpass coaches individuals and makes notes on each student's approach and comprehension of the mathematics. Classmates present their problems and solutions on an overhead projector at the end of the lesson. Two of the presentations appear at the end of this chapter. It is the ability of these children to articulate their thinking and the methods they use which makes clear how much Ms. Malpass has taught them.

The content Ms. Malpass teaches each day addresses the math strands in the California standards in place during that current year. Subjects typically covered include decomposing numbers, fact families, time, money, date and its meaning, color patterns, greater and less than, and fractions. Because students touch on these subjects consistently throughout the year, they not only learn the math skills, but also remember them. She uses the math wall exercises to support the number choices students will select when they approach problem-solving tasks. She is front-loading, and introducing key information in advance of its use, for students who tend to struggle with the word problems.

Prior to coming to Los Alamitos, Ms. Malpass taught in North Carolina where she trained for three years in the practice called Cognitively Guided Instruction (CGI). She willingly shared this approach with her colleagues at Weaver and from other schools in her district. Later, educators from nearby suburban towns and others from schools situated in low-income neighborhoods in both L.A. and Orange counties began coming to observe and learn from her.

Teachers watching Ms. Malpass's demonstrations were stunned by what they had seen. They realized that both they and their students might well be able to achieve so much more than they had previously imagined. Afterwards, many purchased books such as *Children's Mathematics: Cognitively Guided Instruction* (Carpenter *et al.* 2015), watched videos of exemplary teachers, attended training sessions at the county education offices, requested and received coaching from their mentors as they taught this approach, and continued working to hone their skills. They were determined to get the same results with their children as they had observed in Ms. Malpass's room. They wanted to organize their instruction the way she did so that they, too, could teach math standards appropriate for first through third grades in the same lesson. Having their students articulate their understanding of numbers and math problems, as Ms. Malpass's students did, became a goal each longed to reach.

Box 3.3 Pause & Reflect

How did the teacher plan the lesson to match the needs of children in her room? What do you think you might learn from watching a teacher like Ms. Malpass work with her students?

Getting a vision of what can be realized in both teaching and student learning is a powerful motivator for change. Teachers who are initially uncertain about why they should try new things or what to try, can turn completely around and jump at opportunities to learn more after seeing highly successful teachers produce extraordinary results with children in ordinary classrooms. When watching exemplary teachers, other educators can see how to pull students into the content with the force of their passion for the subjects they teach, and ways to engage students in learning through the instructional approaches and activities in use. This desire to emulate what the demonstration teachers do is particularly strong when observers can see a cluster of teachers collaborating across grade levels within the same school using the same impressive methods of instruction. Observers are also drawn to effective and well-documented approaches they can learn in depth later by attending workshops, reading books, and watching videos. They recognize that they and their colleagues can use these resources as they try to become expert instructors who get similarly striking results with their pupils.

Summary

Observing great instructors in action can help teachers shape a vision for what they can do differently to produce significantly better results in student learning. Teachers talk about what they noticed and how it affected them when they visited elementary school classrooms to see extraordinary teachers conducting reading and writing lessons. Observers are particularly impressed by watching a cluster of teachers collaborating across grade levels using the same methods of instruction. Planning in advance of demonstration lessons helps teachers make the most of these learning opportunities. Selecting the most effective instructors to serve as models, setting aside sufficient funding for substitute time, encouraging visitors to attend as school teams, and establishing an etiquette for visitations can contribute to more productive observations.

Reference

Carpenter, Thomas P., Elizabeth Fennema, Megan Loef Franke, Linda Levi, and Susan B. Empson. 2015. *Children's Mathematics: Cognitively Guided Instruction.* Portsmouth, NH: Heinemann.

Appendix A: Janine's Solution

Janine used the number choice (8 + 8). She stands at the projector prepared to write on the overhead sheet with her marker. She begins her explanation:

"First, I put 8 + 8 = 16." She writes the equation on the overhead and then proceeds. "I put one in each group, and then I put two on the side because I used four and there were six."

"Interesting!" Ms. Malpass says. "Which house were you focusing on?"

"The ones place."

"Who can tell us when you are looking at 16, what number is in the ones place?"

Figure 3.1 Janine's First Step in Calculating a Solution to Her Problem

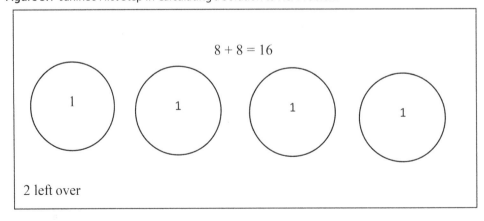

Figure 3.2 Janine's Final Solution

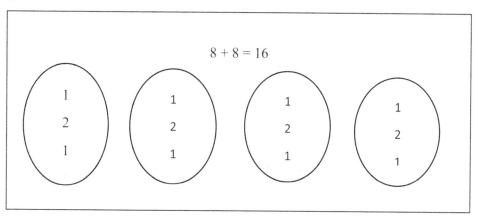

"Six," a student answers.

"So, if I start with the two and add the ones, does it equal six? Two, three, four, five, six. Does it equal six?"

"Yes," they all say.

"Janine, so what have you used?"

"I've used the six. Next, I had a 10, so I put 2, 4, 6, 8," she says as she divides the 10 by twos and allocates two to each of the four circles she has drawn on the sheet. She continues, ". . . and I had two left over. So, I added my twos together and they equaled four."

Janine divides the leftover four into equal groups of one and puts the ones in the circles.

"Next, it said take three out of the four groups." She circles three groups.

"What was in each of those four groups?"

"A one, a two, and a one."

"And that equals what?"

"It equals four. So, I knew 4 + 4 equals 8, plus one more four would equal 11 . . . wait, no . . . 12. So, my answer was 12."

"What does 12 mean?"

"Twelve of them had nuts . . . candies had nuts."

"And what did the other group represent?"

"Candies that didn't have nuts."

Appendix B: Zaidin's Solution

Zaidin came up to share his thinking about the problem using the numbers (18 x 25 + 102). He begins, "Eighteen times 25 equals 450, plus 102 equals 552. The way I knew that was . . . 100 + 450 would be 550, plus 2 is 552."

Zaidin correctly multiplied before completing the addition.

"Could you go back one more step and prove to us that 18 groups of 25 equal 450?"

"Sixteen groups of 25 equal 400 because quarters . . . 25, 50, 75, 100 . . . four groups of 25. Eight is 200. Twelve is 300. Sixteen is 400 and then I have two more, so that would be 450. And then, I, so I took 400 out of it and I put 100 in each group of my 400. Then I had 152 left. I took the 100 out and put 25 in each group, and then I had 52 left."

Looking proud and with an impish grin, he proceeds to explain. "So now I know about a deck of cards. It has 52 cards and 13 cards are in each suit and there's four suits. And I needed to split it into four. So, it's 13. The answer is 13. So now I have 100, 25, 13. Five and three equals eight and 20 and 10 equals 30, so your answer is 30. One hundred plus zero is 100. So, your answer is 138. So, three 138s is . . . I don't know the answer yet. Eight plus eight plus eight is 24. So, I put down the 4 and carry the 20."

"What did he carry, everybody?"

"Twenty," answers the class.

"How is he representing the 20?"

"With a 2."

Understanding place value, that the 2 represents a 20 in this case, is a principle the teacher continually reinforces with the students.

Zaidin goes on: "So, 2 + 3 + 3 + 3."

"Can you use that in tens language?"

"Yeah, 20 + 30 + 30 + 30."

"What would be the most efficient way to add that up?"

"Thirty + 30 + 30 equals 90, plus 20 equals 110. I have 10, so I'm going to put down my 10 and carry my hundred. So, 100 + 100 + 100 + 100 = 400. So, the answer is 414."

"What does 414 represent?"

"How many candies have nuts? Then, there's 138 without nuts."

Questions and compliments from the class follow. Zaidin's work on the overhead is below.

Figure 3.3 Zaidin's Calculations and Solution to His Problem

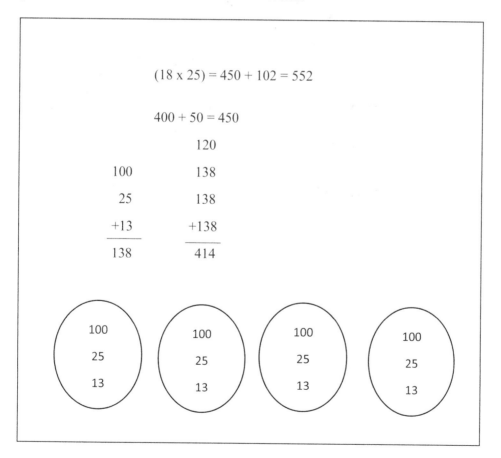

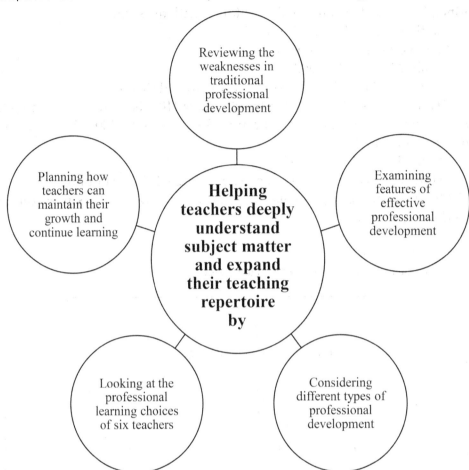

4

Go Deep into Content and Methodology

I don't think our district really offers us much. They don't offer enough variety. It's kind of like all six schools, all teachers, all grade levels need to do the same thing and be on the same page. It's like putting a ceiling on us as far as what we are learning. I think they want us all to be the same and I really fight that. I like individuality. I love expression and personality in the kids. I love that in other people and professionals as well. When people are genuinely themselves, and they have a comfort level with that and an ownership of it, you can gain from that because they have different strengths and weaknesses. Instead of having everybody do the same thing repeatedly, to me it's just not open enough. I wish they had more choices available for us.

Laura, a first-grade teacher with more than
20 years of experience

Professional development has a terrible reputation among many educators. They have a laundry list of complaints about school and district workshops, and top of the list is that all teachers are treated the same regardless of their knowledge or experience. Whole faculties are required to attend school-wide training sessions and teachers have little choice with respect to their professional learning plan. Those who have the skill to teach the course themselves must sit and listen alongside others who are unfamiliar with the material.

Other teachers will sometimes complain that professional development is too theoretical. While they want to know why a teaching method gets superior results, sessions dominated by theory and low on practical application feel like a waste of their precious time. They want to learn something they can use. They tire of hearing from "experts" with little current classroom experience. These presenters fail to convince the audience that they are intimately familiar with the day-to-day challenges of the classroom and the difficulties of using the methods being touted. Teachers respond enthusiastically when ideas and approaches have been thoroughly tested in classrooms and the trainers know the ins and outs of reaching students using the materials introduced.

Too often, professional development fails to acknowledge that how one teaches is influenced by what is taught. Training can be about methods alone, with no connection to the subject matter and skills students are to learn. More effective training centers on one specific content and the teaching approaches appropriate for instruction of that material.

Most problematic is that there is often no follow-up to help teachers delve deeper into the nuances of the content and pedagogy introduced in workshops. Little support or coaching is offered in the classroom as teachers present substantially different subject matter or attempt to use new methods. As a result, training notes and materials get shelved or forgotten in the busy and demanding lives of teachers.

What educators need to improve their craft is a different mission for professional development and a revitalized conception of how teachers learn best. The mission of professional development should be to help teachers at each stage of their careers, giving them the tools and training to advance from novice toward higher levels of expertise. Professional learning, then, should be thought of as a process of growth taking place throughout one's work life. The assumptions are that educational methods and our understanding of student learning change over time because of new research information and our increasing aspirations for more advanced student performance. One aim of professional development, then, should be to offer individuals a wide array of learning experiences from which to choose to continuously advance their teaching skills and the achievements of students as their understandings change about best practices in teaching and how children learn.

Features of Effective Professional Development

Effective professional development which results in implementation of new material and the use of more successful teaching methods should include several features. Among these are choice or self-determination in creating a professional learning plan, a focus on one subject and a related teaching approach simultaneously, intensity and duration of training substantial enough to ensure full understanding of the pedagogy and subject matter, plus opportunities to practice and revise new approaches in the classroom with the support of a coach.

Choice

Experienced and competent teachers prefer workshops they choose themselves to expand their repertoire and help them achieve even greater success with students. Their professional development trajectory is self-directed and individualized to fit their specific needs. Teachers who set their own professional goals and select the training to support their learning are more committed to their plans and own those choices as compared with educators who have little say in what and how they will be taught. The power of teachers marking out their own path to progress and opting in to a process of change and growth can be magical and can completely turn around any negative sentiments they may have had in the past about professional learning opportunities.

Choice and the personalizing of professional development does present potential problems for school and district leaders. Principals and superintendents concerned about coherence in the district's instructional practices may struggle to find a balance between reaching that goal and mobilizing teacher ownership of continuous improvement. That balance is often achieved when groups of teachers within schools and districts work together on a shared goal of their choice. When teachers join collectively to learn about and perfect ways to teach that stimulate and sustain student engagement and achievement, all parties will benefit, including the individual instructor, the school and district, and the students involved.

Focus

Going deeper into subject matter and exploring how the content can best be taught takes time, attention, and practice. To fully understand the material and be able to predict the many ways students will respond to learning it themselves requires focus on one subject for an extended period of time. The competing demands and distractions at almost any school site make focus difficult to achieve. Principals and teachers are stretched by multiple agendas promoted by the district, the state, and the federal government. It is no wonder that teachers tire of a parade of initiatives quickly introduced with little support. Trying out a new practice is an up-and-down process which takes time to get right. The goal for professional development should be for teachers to use more effective teaching methods and to be continuously refining these approaches until they succeed in improving student learning.

Achieving this goal necessitates doing less, but with a greater depth of understanding. One subject and relevant teaching methods should be the teacher's professional learning focus for at least a year, if not two or three, before moving on to other content.

Intensity and Duration

In a rigorous review of research about how professional development affects student achievement, Yoon and colleagues (2007) examined nine experimental studies meeting the standards of the What Works Clearinghouse in Washington, D.C. A common characteristic of the professional development in these studies was a focus on an effective curriculum or instructional model for an average of 49 hours during the year. Eight of the programs incorporated follow-up support with initial training. Similarly, the Council of Chief State School Officers (CCSSO) published a review of evaluations of professional development programs (Blank, de las Alas, and Smith 2008) for math and science which showed improved student outcomes. Characteristic of these programs was a focus on content and content-pedagogy for a duration of 45 to 300 hours a year, with most having more than 100 hours of professional learning. Along with substantial time spent in learning, the programs featured collaborative activities such as mentoring, follow-up training in content and pedagogy for groups of teachers, lesson study, and learning activities in grade-level teams.

Practice

Effective professional training programs also incorporate opportunities for teachers to practice and revise the unfamiliar material and approaches to it. Practice with a mentor—one who helps teachers be accountable for application of new practices, offers encouragement and assistance in implementation, and provides feedback—is especially important when the overall goal is to bring about changes in teaching and student learning.

Types of Professional Development

Professional development happens during national or local conferences, school-based workshops, observations of teaching, laboratory classrooms, one-to-one coaching, study groups, and in many other formats such as on-line courses and professional books. The value of conferences, workshops, and lab classes are described below. Details on observations appear in Chapter 3, coaching in Chapter 5, and study groups in Chapters 5 and 6.

Conferences and Workshops

One-time workshops at conferences or in school settings, despite their poor reputation for getting results, can be initial sources of inspiration and vehicles for introducing unfamiliar teaching methods and educational research. They are often the starting point from which teachers can choose to build a more substantial professional learning plan. For educators who are ready to try out more effective methods in the classroom, but are uncertain what approaches are most likely to be productive, attending national subject-matter conferences or regional workshops featuring distinguished authors and eminent researchers may provide useful information and suggest the next steps to take in professional learning.

Teachers in the Art of Teaching fellowship regularly attend an annual conference which features practitioners of effective teaching approaches in reading, writing, mathematics, social studies, and science. These participants say they feel invigorated after this initial exposure to so many new ideas, and many find at least one teaching method particularly appealing. They begin to envision themselves presenting curriculum and instruction more rigorous and complex than they have previously offered their students.

During the year and into the following summer, these teachers continue studying a subject by cycling back to additional conferences and extended workshops focused on the one topic they chose to pursue. We found that most are typically drawn to approaches which challenge students' thinking. Examples are Reader's Workshop, Writer's Workshop, Cognitively Guided Instruction, Great Books' Shared Inquiry, and the Library of Congress's offerings on uses of primary sources to teach social studies and literature.

Reader's Workshop and Writer's Workshop stem from the research of Don Graves on writing development and Lucy Calkin's Reading and Writing Project. Calkins established a think tank and training institute at Columbia University to show teachers how to help children become good writers, and later, how to teach reading. She is the author of more than 20 books, including *The Art of Teaching Writing* (1994). The writing workshop method makes students aware of what successful adult writers do, such as draft, revise, edit, and publish. Similarly, the reading workshop method introduces the habits of good readers, such as predicting or asking oneself questions about the text. Teachers model reading skills before the entire class. Then they confer regularly with children individually and in small groups to teach specific writing and reading skills.

Teachers with a passion for math often choose to learn about Cognitively Guided Instruction. CGI was originally explored by Thomas Carpenter and others on his research team (2015) at the University of Wisconsin, with funding from the National Science Foundation and the U.S. Department of Education's Office of Educational Research and Improvement. CGI helps teachers identify what is easy and what is hard for children to comprehend about mathematics. Emphasis is placed on finding what students do best and then building upon that. It is not a curriculum, but it is based on the premise that younger students can learn unifying ideas of mathematics that are foundational to both arithmetic and algebra.

The Great Books Foundation draws teachers to their professional development on "shared inquiry" to learn how to teach students to dive into the subtle meanings of text, and debate points raised in reading materials. Others seek out summer training at the Library of Congress to learn how to use primary sources to examine and explain history, or how to teach literature using online resources. Workshops emphasize ways that teachers can help students collect evidence and draw conclusions using these valuable materials.

The appeal of approaches like these may be explained in a few ways. One draw is that these methods emphasize teaching students to understand complex material deeply. Teaching for understanding is difficult to master, and learning how to do it well is a reasonable next step for good teachers to take along the road to excellence. Also, if teachers observe great instructors using these methods, they are awed by what the students can achieve. They want to emulate these superb educators. A third attraction is that books and training seminars are available which explain the rationale for these approaches and detail ways to implement them. Teachers have tangible tools to help them learn to become far more accomplished at teaching reading, writing, math, and social studies.

Laboratory Classes

Lab classes are another form of professional development which aids teachers in developing expertise using new practices. A key feature of these learning experiences is that they involve groups of teachers observing lessons taught by colleagues or master teachers in classrooms with students. Labs include a time for pre-planning and/or debriefing so that the visiting teachers and hosting teachers can learn with and from each other.

One type of lab class is for teachers who, in the early stages of using a new practice with their students, want to learn from their peers who are also struggling to try out the approach. For example, watching model teachers who have mastered Reader's Workshop is one thing; seeing what instruction may look like when teachers first introduce the program is something else. Visiting teachers want to observe what the first year or two of implementation of a different teaching strategy might entail; and they want to discuss with colleagues how to overcome the problems in their practice that many of them have in common.

Teachers at a host school invite groups of teachers from other schools to observe their teaching. At the end of an observation, visitors and demonstration teachers, aided by a facilitator who is expert in the teaching method, comment on the strengths and potential problems in the instruction. Together, the group discusses which elements of the lesson should be preserved and generates ideas on how to overcome less effective aspects of the teaching. Observations may continue next in another teacher's class and then be followed by discussion. Because labs involve people like themselves implementing new teaching methods with students in classrooms, the lessons learned are vivid and real for the teachers.

A second example of a lab class is one taught at the University of Michigan School of Education by Deborah Lowenberg Ball. A classroom full of fifth-graders from the Ypsilanti schools comes to the Elementary Mathematics Laboratory on the college campus, where during the summer they will wrestle with concepts such as "equal parts" and "the whole," as Ball probes their thinking by asking questions. Her emphasis is on reasoning and problem-solving, respectful argumentation, and critical analysis. Teachers attend the lab class in the morning where they discuss the lesson to be presented before class begins and help refine the lesson plan. Then, they observe instruction. After class, they debrief, ask questions, and examine student work. They spend their afternoons in workshops where they identify the purposes and types of discussion used in mathematics classrooms, plus build a toolbox of instructional techniques to conduct relevant discussions with children.

Another kind of lab class is one led by a master teacher in a local school setting. Its purpose is to help teachers understand more thoroughly the components of a teaching approach and the content taught through a process of co-constructing a lesson, observing instruction, and analyzing how students respond. A lab held at Park Western Place Elementary School in the Los Angeles Unified School District is a perfect example. Two dozen teachers came from a variety of schools to learn how students think about mathematics and how to construct lessons that build upon children's understandings. They arrived in pairs and small groups so that when they return to their schools, they can continue their conversations and learn more together.

Consulting teacher Joan Case led the lab day on the topics of equal sharing and fractions. The first activity of the day was to brainstorm word problems for third-graders using the expression $(26 \div 4)$. The teachers worked in groups to develop the four problems below. Ms. Case then led them in a discussion of how each problem might be understood by the children:

1. Marie had 26 candies to share with three friends. How many candies does each person get if she shares them equally? How many are left over? (*Members of the group asked whether the problem needs to be more precise and whether students will know that Marie is also getting candies along with her three friends.*)

2. Ron has 26 pieces of pizza. He shares them equally with himself and three friends. How many slices does each person have? How many pieces are left over? (*Teachers point out that the two leftover pieces could each be divided in half to fair share all 26 pieces.*)

3. X has 26 pieces of Rice Krispies Treats. X shares all of it equally with himself and three other friends. How much does each person have? (*The group talks about how this problem uses partitive division to introduce fractions as the two leftover Rice Krispies Treats can continue to be shared by the four sharers by creating fractional amounts.*)

4. Mari is making four necklaces for her friends. She has 26 beads to share equally to make each necklace. How many beads are on a necklace and how many are left over? (*Teachers mention that because the two remaining beads cannot easily be divided in half, the problem does not lend itself to introducing fractions in the same way that problem number 3 does.*)

Ms. Case reviews important ideas about posing problems. One is to start by asking the children to read and deconstruct the word problem to clarify any ambiguities and make sure students understand what the problem asks them to do. Another is to use stories about equal sharing of concrete objects when introducing fractions because these make sense to kids. For example, start with stories of clay, ribbons, or Krispies. Save more abstract concepts like "miles" for later. Begin with whole numbers and let the fractions come out of solving the problem. A different thought is to begin with two or four sharers to allow for the problem to be solved using halves and/or fourths only. Finally, she suggests that thinking in advance about how kids will solve the problem will help the teachers determine the numbers to use.

The visiting teachers join Ms. Case in the third-grade room where she presents a lesson and each of them takes notes on one or two students.

She begins with, "Do you know what a Rice Krispies Treat is? What is it like?"

The children tell her what they know.

"Today's story," she says, "is about you sharing Rice Krispies Treats with three friends. You have a plate of ten Rice Krispies Treats and you want to share them equally. How many treats does each of you get so that you use it all up? We will collect your work."

She asks questions to check whether they understand what to do next, and then they get to work.

When time is up, the teachers collect the student work and return to the auditorium. Ms. Case has them look at the 22 papers and identify three different approaches students used to solve the problem so that they can understand the details of students' thinking. The three methods they describe are:

1. One student drew ten boxes and divided them in half. She tried to find groups of two for each child and kept getting eight total. She abandoned that method. She later cut the two remaining Krispies into four parts but could not describe what to call the fractional parts.
2. Another child wrote 4/2, but wasn't familiar with the term so described it as one-half. Then, he wrote 4 x 2=8.
3. A third student tried to do an array, but wasn't sure what to do. She was using trial and error to find a solution.

Talking about what they noticed while they watched the children working, the teachers said things like:

"Kids need time to think. Silence, starring into space, is thinking time. We shouldn't interrupt them."

"Some students are able to pass out wholes only."

"One child cut all ten Krispies into fourths but didn't know what to call them."

"Some used the word 'half' for the two remaining Krispies, but then they ended up with 12 pieces and couldn't explain it."

"Some don't distinguish between wholes and parts."

"This problem pushed their learning because it was challenging and students worked to make sense of it."

The group continues talking about the mathematics and the key ideas in this lesson. The content standards state that students will understand that $a \div b = a/b$. Students will see that $1 \div 4 = 1/4$ or $10 \div 4 = 10/4$. Together they discuss what they learned about the students' understanding of fractional quantities and what they were still curious about. From this information, they plan what problem to pose next to the children.

The teachers return to the third-grade room to watch Ms. Case introduce a continuation of the math lesson. She tells the children that there are three blocks of clay for four kids and asks them how much clay each one gets if you share the three bars equally. Again, the students get to work reading the problem, drawing representations of it, and writing how they arrived at their solutions. Again, the visiting teachers take notes on individuals as they work. At the end of this problem-solving period, teachers return to the auditorium to examine the student work and decide which work will be shared with the whole class. Then, all go back to the class to conclude the day with a share-out by the students.

Ms. Case asks Chloe to come up to the board to draw and describe her solution for the class. Chloe draws three squares of clay. She divides the first two in half. Ms. Case asks the class to predict how Chloe will divide the third bar.

One student replies, "I predict she is going to cut it in half and then half again and give it to each one."

And, in fact, as predicted, Chloe does divide the third bar into fourths.

"Why did it work for Chloe to cut the last bar into four pieces?" asks the teacher.

"It is fair," answers one child.

"Our first piece of clay . . . how much did each person get?"

"One-half," answers the class.

Pointing to one of the four squares in the third bar of clay, Ms. Case asks, "Is this also one-half of the bar of clay?"

"No!" is the response.

"How do you know?"

"It looks bigger on the first clay piece," says one child.

"If you added another of these pieces, it would be a half," speculates another student.

Figure 4.1 The Portion of the Block of Clay that the Teacher Asks Students to Name

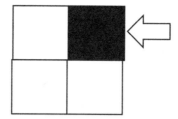

Pointing to a part of the third bar of clay, the teacher asks, "Anyone know what we call this?"

"One fourth," answers one child.

"One quarter," answers another.

Ms. Case asks Jorge to present another strategy. She has the class talk with a neighbor about how each thinks Jorge will cut the clay. The students chat in pairs and then present their ideas.

"Diagonal? I'm not sure."

"He'll cut it in four pieces," tries a different student.

The teacher asks a student to come up and cut a bar into four pieces. "That was the first block. Now what?"

After talking among themselves, one child imagines that he will cut them all the same.

Another boy suggests that every kid would get three pieces. He comes up to show the class by numbering the squares to represent which piece goes to

Figure 4.2 A Student Divides Three Blocks of Clay into Four Equal Pieces

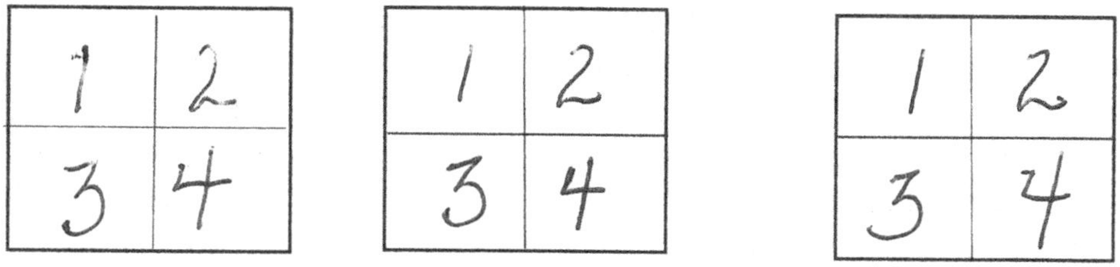

1	2
3	4

1	2
3	4

1	2
3	4

each of the four children. "One goes to one. Two goes to two. Three goes to three. Four goes to four."

"Very smart!" says a classmate.

The visitors return to the auditorium to talk about what the presentations by the students accomplished. A few teachers had been worried that the problem was too hard for the students. Some children didn't get it and didn't finish the problem. But through the share-out, these same teachers conclude that a great deal was accomplished. Ms. Case remarks that the kids tell us what to talk about and do next. She suggests they think first about what the group needs, consider the goals of the lesson, and then go looking for student work to be shared. One teacher comments that asking students to predict what a child did to solve a problem helped to keep everyone engaged. Teachers left the lab class at the end of the day having considered the mathematics more thoroughly than before and having practiced many planning steps to take for a lesson such as this.

Box 4.1   Pause & Reflect

Which formats for professional learning are used at your school or in your district? How do each of them contribute to continuous improvement of teaching? What more do you think could be done to improve teaching through professional learning opportunities?

Putting It All Together

Susan Gehn's students at Monona Grove School District in Wisconsin were part of the original research on CGI conducted by Thomas Carpenter and colleagues (2015). She retired after 31 years of teaching and now offers CGI training nation-wide as a consultant with the Teachers Development Group. Her description of her work with schools illustrates how to put together a comprehensive package of professional learning with many components, such as workshops, reading of research on how students learn math, practice with children, collaborative work, and follow-up coaching at school sites:

Our professional development is ideal because it takes place over time, focuses on kids, and teachers see it in action in the classroom. It usually begins with four days in the summer where participants learn about the research on children's mathematical thinking and the stages of development they go through. The participants interview kids and watch videos of children solving problems. In grade-level groups, they write two to three problems of their own to try out with their students when they return to their schools. Teachers read the text and work in small groups to summarize the material by writing a description of the big idea within a reading. Most important are the three follow-up days during the school year where they visit a classroom, interview children, examine the data, and make instructional decisions. They also decide which student work to share in the classroom. Teachers come up with a goal based upon the interviews and develop questions to ask the children.

Del Mar Union School District in California started putting all the components of comprehensive professional learning together years ago after they decided to make the improvement of elementary school mathematics instruction a priority. With Victoria Jacobs, who was then at San Diego State University and has since moved to the University of North Carolina at Greensboro, they developed an initial three-year plan for mathematics which featured choice, focus, intensity, duration, and practice. Now going into its seventh year, the plan incorporates a variety of professional development formats, including workshops, student interviews, classroom observation, collaborative work, and team coaching. The district made time available for teachers to work together.

The goal was to train every elementary school teacher in the district in the Cognitively Guided Instruction approach to teaching mathematics. The district had too many teachers at eight schools to train all in the first year, so they rolled the professional learning offerings out over time. By the third year of implementation, after hearing from colleagues what they had learned, all remaining teachers were eager to participate. Within one more year, all were on board with CGI, at varying levels.

Within a few years, the program had expanded to include something for everyone, including new hires. The offerings in the sixth year of the program were composed of Year 1 and Year 2 content training for new hires and/or teachers who changed grade levels, and then some courses for primary grade instructors and others for those teaching upper grades. Teachers were divided into cohorts based upon their years of training. Cohorts 1 and 2 were made up of teachers who were first in the district to receive training and more advanced in their study of CGI. Cohorts 3 and 4 were formed by teachers who had completed three to four years of content training, but were not as experienced as teachers in Cohorts 1 and 2. Teachers in Cohort 1 and 2 chose two sessions, and those teachers in Cohorts 3 and 4 chose up to four sessions from a list of courses. These lists differed for different grade levels. Sessions from which the K-3 teachers made their selections included titles such as the following:

- Understanding and Encouraging Invented Algorithms and Notation – Teachers refine their understanding of invented algorithms and their importance to students. They explore how to encourage the development of invented algorithms during instruction, how to notate them effectively, how to support student flexibility in using different strategies and promote student understanding of different algorithms.
- Fractions – This session supports the development of fractional reasoning for students below third grade. Teachers practice choosing problems, numbers, and questions.
- Development of Base Ten/Place Value – A foundational understanding for primary students. This session is about how to build base ten/place value understanding through problem-solving. Topics include effective problem types, activities that build place value understanding, important ways to notate, and the use of equations to support student learning.

In addition, the teachers could choose from four courses in which collaboration with colleagues and/or facilitation by teacher leaders were part of the design:

- Collaboration Activity (with a partner) – Teachers collaborate with a colleague to examine children's mathematical thinking. Partners observe each other and discuss their experiences. Teachers sort student work, plan the student sharing session, and shape the next lesson. Teachers are provided with a structure to guide the day's learning.
- Grade Level Team Collaboration (all members of a grade level) – Teams focus on a problem-solving lesson and a student sharing session. A teacher leader, principal, or district staff member facilitates.
- Grade Level Embedded Day – Embedded days start with sorting student work and the development of a new problem to use in a grade-level teacher's classroom. Students solve the problem and their work is collected. Participants sort the work, plan next steps, and observe a sharing session led by a teacher in the group. A facilitator is provided.

◆ Interview Students – Teachers interview students in their classroom on day one. On day two, grade-level teachers discuss what data from the interviews tell them and how to use that data to plan next steps.

The district's careful planning is revealed in three more strategic moves. First, they engaged everyone in CGI training. Principals and district administrators attended training so that they could understand what and how teachers were teaching and support them in their efforts. This move put teachers and administrators on the same page philosophically with respect to math instruction and helped develop a common language about math education among all district staff.

Second, they trained cadres of teacher leaders to assist in future work. First, they chose six teachers who had completed three or four years of CGI training to become apprentices to Dinah Brown, Coordinator of Curriculum and Instruction. For three years, they worked beside her and another presenter as they conducted professional learning. At the end of the apprenticeship, these six will lead the learning sessions on their own. Another 25 teachers make up the teacher leadership group. These individuals have received specialized professional learning in content and working with other teachers to facilitate Grade Level Collaboration Days. In that role, they model instruction and collaboration with peers, as well as lead discussion sessions.

Third, parents needed to know how teaching mathematics was changing and why. District staff held 16 parent nights the first year of the program, and another set of parent nights in year six, to explain what they were trying to achieve and give parents examples of what students would be doing. Keeping parents in the loop continues.

Consistency is critical if schools and districts are aiming for excellence. Superintendent Holly McClurg and the Assistant Superintendent for Instructional Services, Shelly Petersen, provided that consistency for Del Mar Union. In the first two years of CGI training, the district had hired Dinah Brown as a consultant to implement their program. In year three, they brought her onto the staff full time to continue and expand the work she had begun. For some half-dozen years, the district devoted its full attention to helping teachers improve student achievement and understanding of mathematics. The results showed up in their already-high test scores. In the first year of the state's Smarter Balance standardized test results, Del Mar Union achieved a ranking near the top in the state and many more of its students reached the "exceeding" category of performance as compared with the state or the county. The results are evident in the day-to-day behavior of students as well. As Dinah Brown describes it, "Every teacher's instruction has changed. Teachers tell us that they can't believe what our kids know now."

Six Teachers on their Own Paths

The personal professional development plans of six teachers at one school in the Art of Teaching offer a different example of how a comprehensive learning program designed by the teachers themselves can work. These six participated in more than 130 hours of professional development each year for two years to jump-start their pursuit of excellence. While most of their time was spent with a mentor once or twice each week in coaching and planning sessions, they still demonstrate how various forms of professional development support teacher learning. These six also show that even when teachers choose their own paths of professional learning, it does not mean that they need to learn in isolation. They chose subjects of great value to improving student achievement and they joined with their colleagues to learn a broader repertoire of methods for teaching those subjects.

All six teachers attended a Saturday conference in September to get inspired and collect ideas for the new school year. Two of those who chose math as the subject on which they would focus went the next month to Los Alamitos Unified School District to participate in two school-based institutes. An institute gives teachers the opportunity to observe a teaching practice done by different teachers across several grade levels. Expert instructors at Weaver Elementary demonstrated Cognitively Guided Instruction. The institute at McGaugh Elementary centered on Contexts for Learning Mathematics lessons. Shortly thereafter, these two teachers hosted a CGI lab day at their own school. With visiting instructors in their rooms, they taught lessons under the watchful eye of math consultant Angela Chan Turrou from UCLA, who gave feedback during and after the instruction. The hosts and visitors then discussed successes and challenges they were having as they implemented CGI in their own schools. In January, they went to a CGI dinner meeting for teachers new to CGI and more experienced colleagues. This was led by teachers who had been using this approach for several years. In March, they saw CGI in action again at two schools in their own district. For good measure, they also participated in language arts meetings, including an evening gathering to share ideas on Reader's Workshop and a separate training session on that subject.

The other four teachers, who chose reading as their focus, attended several events including "Advanced Reader's Workshop" and "Advanced Writer's Workshop," Junior Great Books training, and two language arts lab classes where teachers still learning the workshop technique demonstrated reading instruction. They also went to the UCLA Lab School to observe classes and learn more about Reader's Workshop from members of that faculty. Toward the end of the year, the four joined a language arts gathering to have dinner and share with other teachers the details of their evolving practices. Taking advantage of reading and writing seminars sponsored by other organizations, one of the four participated in a Daily 5 Webinar and a Café 5 Conference led by the authors who call themselves "The Sisters." A second teacher chose a training session at the UCLA Lab School on how to use primary sources when teaching history and reading.

Given the time and resources allocated to them, these teachers made full use of the best learning opportunities available. After two years of adding to their knowledge of the ways students learn, adopting unique methods to teach specific content, being coached, and studying with their colleagues on campus, all six had become more masterful in their own teaching. They also helped change the culture of their school into an environment in which teachers work together to solve problems and strengthen each other's practice.

Continuous Study

There is much more to professional learning than an intensive focus on one new practice for a year or two. Masterful teaching takes years to polish. Sustaining and refining the methodology that the teacher has recently added to his or her repertoire takes additional attention, practice, and study. Eventually, after becoming highly skilled in one subject, each educator will want to move on to refine the particular teaching approach to a second, third, or fourth content focus.

Joining a regional or national subject-matter organization is a good way to continue hearing about new research in the field and staying abreast of curricular changes. National conferences sponsored by these organizations offer refresher courses to keep educators up to date.

Teachers involved in study groups at their own schools can continue their involvement whether the meetings are held during school hours or after work. If the topics are important to the participants and the groups are facilitated well, teachers are often reluctant to give up these times of opportunity to dialogue with their peers.

Others attending specialized workshops or classroom observations may have met colleagues from other schools within their district or across different districts that they have grown to respect and know personally. There is a strong pull to stay connected with those who share the same interests and are wrestling with the same issues in teaching. Teachers have organized their own networks around topics like Reader's Workshop or Shared Inquiry where groups of 8–12 of them meet regularly to describe what they have learned about implementing these strategies. They bring student work to discuss what their pupils have achieved and brainstorm next steps in teaching. They develop curriculum together, share professional readings, and operate as a support system to keep each other accountable for continuing to improve their instruction.

Districts and other groups have assisted teachers by hosting dinner meetings or special events where teachers who are expert in a practice lead a meeting for any other teachers in their district who want to offer their expertise as well as explore more about the subject under discussion. All that is needed is a place to meet, some food and drink to make people feel at home, an invitation list as diverse as possible, and a teacher or two who are excellent facilitators to lead the meetings and create opportunities for teachers to share what they know and what they want to learn with each other.

Lab classes hosted by individual schools or the district can also be open to teachers at all levels of expertise in the teaching methods being demonstrated. In this way, highly competent teachers keep refining their work while learning side by side with those who are new to the practice.

Today's online learning opportunities are enormous. Professional development courses matching any teacher's interest are available for those who want to communicate with and hear from others in the field.

No matter what the format, continuous study requires a commitment of time and energy to professional growth. Continuous study changes teaching from a routine into an evolving and always improving profession. Learning with and from colleagues, and constantly polishing one's own craft to become increasingly successful with the students, are energizing and renewing endeavors which make a teaching career truly satisfying.

Summary

Traditional professional development is ineffective and seldom results in implementation of new content or methods. A different view of how teachers learn, and a new format of comprehensive professional learning is needed. More effective professional development offers features such as choice, focus, intensity, duration, and practice. Formats may vary and include traditional conferences and workshops, observations, coaching, study groups, and lab classes. Continuous study and learning with and from colleagues can revitalize a teaching career and result in greater levels of student achievement.

Resources

Professional development resources mentioned in this chapter can be accessed on the websites of the parent organizations:

- ◆ Examples of superb teaching can be found on video at the Cotsen Foundation for the Art of Teaching at http://cotsen.org/topic/thoughts-on-teaching-excellence/videos/videos-of-teaching/ (retrieved October 31, 2017).
- ◆ The Great Books Foundation describes the Shared-Inquiry process at https://www.greatbooks.org/about/what-is-shared-inquiry (retrieved November 11, 2017).
- ◆ Information about the Library of Congress' Teaching with Primary Sources program and access to related resources are available at http://www.loc.gov/teachers/tps/ (retrieved October 31, 2017).
- ◆ Information about Reader's and Writer's Workshop methods, materials, and events are detailed at the Teachers College site, http://www.readingandwritingproject.org/ (retrieved October 31, 2017).
- ◆ Training and coaching in Cognitively Guided Instruction is offered by the Teachers Development Group: https://www.teachersdg.org/ (retrieved October 31, 2017).

References

Blank, Rolf K., Nina de las Alas, and Carlise Smith. 2008. *Does Teacher Professional Development Have Effects on Teaching and Learning? Analysis of Evaluation Findings from Programs for Mathematics and Science Teachers in 14 States.* Retrieved from http://www.ccsso.org/documents/2008/does_teacher_professional_development_2008.pdf.

Calkins, Lucy McCormick. 1994. *The Art of Teaching Writing.* Portsmouth, NH: Heinemann.

Carpenter, Thomas P., Elizabeth Fennema, Megan Loef Franke, Linda Levi, and Susan B. Empson. 2015. *Children's Mathematics: Cognitively Guided Instruction.* Portsmouth, NH: Heinemann.

Yoon, Kwang Suk, Teresa Duncan, Silvia Wen-Yu Lee, Beth Scarloss, and Kathy L. Shapley. 2007. "Reviewing the Evidence on How Teacher Professional Development Affects Student Achievement." *Issues & Answers. REL 2007-No.* 033. Retrieved 3 November 2017 from http://www.ies.ed.gov/ncee/edlabs/regions/southwest/pdf/rel_2007033.pdf.

Showing what teachers value about their mentors and coaches

Outlining training for mentors and coaches

Understanding the role of the mentor–coach by

Defining what a mentor is and what a coach is

Giving an example of the complexities of mentoring

Describing what mentors and coaches do

5

Practice with a Mentor–Coach

When we asked participants in the Art of Teaching which aspect of professional development had the greatest impact on their teaching, a common response was "having a mentor to plan, collaborate, and teach with." Working with an intellectual partner can stimulate self-improvement. In a survey, one mentee wrote, "Trying new practices is hard and having a mentor holds me accountable and helps me keep pushing myself even when it is hard or uncomfortable." Another mentee commented, "Teaching can sometimes be isolating and thankless. It has been enjoyable to have someone else in the room to coach me and support me. It's especially fun to have someone there to celebrate the students' successes." Quotes like these give a glimpse into why teachers value their mentors and the coaching process so much.

Why Coaching Is So Important

Even exciting, relevant, and useful training sessions can have little lasting effect on what teachers do in classrooms, because what they need most is support as they transfer this new knowledge into daily practice. Typically, only 10 percent of teachers implement what they hear about in workshops (Bush 1984, 226). There are many reasons for this, including the ever-present demands on teachers' time. School schedules are such that American elementary school teachers spend most of the school day in front of children. Assisting students, meeting with parents, preparing lessons, attending mandated training sessions, completing paperwork, and other jobs consume the few remaining work hours and a good amount of their own time. Tasks like these and the pressures of managing classroom activities and behavior leave instructors with little excess energy for trying out new methods. In addition, the array of new expectations that schools and districts place on teachers every year makes it difficult to stay focused and persist while attempting to integrate new teaching approaches. The difficulty of shedding old habits while trying to master new practices makes successful implementation of what teachers hear about in workshops unlikely without support and encouragement. This is especially true as teachers begin trying out a different way of presenting material or introducing new concepts. A predictable, temporary slump in performance may occur as they learn to use the unfamiliar methods. Fear of failing their students during this awkward stage can result in teachers abandoning their efforts and falling back instead on the routines they know best.

When the same workshops are followed up by coaches working in classrooms, showing teachers how to apply the information and practices just introduced to them, the implementation rate goes up to 95 percent (Bush 1984, 226). A research review by Yoon and colleagues (2007) showed that eight of nine different studies of professional development which resulted in positive impacts on student learning included follow-up support for teachers after training sessions. Coaching is essential if a school or district hopes to have teachers use and eventually master methods and content introduced briefly in workshops.

Beth Pesnell, the math and science curriculum specialist for the K-8 grades in the Rogers Public Schools system in Arkansas, makes clear that:

> Professional development is not a one and done kind of thing. We have had Academic Facilitators in our schools for 13 years. We started with literacy coaches at each building and then added additional coaches for math. When you look at what elementary teachers are expected to do across subjects, it is a lot. The focus of facilitators is to help teachers based on what they need, as well as to assist the school and the district to move our agendas forward.
>
> Our district has participated in sustained mathematics training for our K-5 grade teachers since 2009. Cognitively Guided Instruction in Math, which our K-2 teachers attend, and Extending Children's Mathematics for our grades three to five teachers, are three-year professional development classes designed to help teachers elicit student mathematical thinking. Each year, participants attend a three- to four-day session in the summer and then two to four follow-up days

during the year. Our mathematics coaches have all participated in this professional development, as well, allowing them to support the teachers in their journey. You can't expect teachers to be masters of the subject at the end of a summer's training. You can't just leave them to their own devices. I have heard that it takes something like more than 100 hours for professional development to make a difference. It needs to be embedded and sustained. This kind of support is so important. The teacher needs to be invested in it. Professional learning should be something that they value, not something done to them, but work done with and beside them.

The Difference between a Mentor and a Coach

The term "mentor" is frequently used to describe a relationship in which a knowledgeable person supports a colleague by devoting time and attention to the development of skills and acquisition of critical information in that person. A business mentor is usually one who brings along a co-worker from an early stage as a relative novice to mastery of a field. The mentor helps individuals traverse the rough waters in the business environment and aids their mentees in developing the skills and acumen to succeed.

Mentors, as I use the term throughout this book, are champions of any age with the expertise to assist colleagues in advancing in their careers. They are responsible for helping others strengthen their practice and reach their professional goals. At the same time, they are advocates for a teaching profession in which educators engage in continuous improvement throughout their careers, and have opportunities to wrestle with the problems of their practice with others and share the joys and insights they are gaining.

The term "coach" is often used as a synonym for a mentor, though there are many different styles of coaching. Aguilar (2013, 19) makes clear what coaches should not do. These tasks include training others to teach exactly like the coach does, or evaluating and reporting on whether teachers are using a program. Coaching should not be used as a fix for ineptitude or to provide therapy. Instead, like a mentor, a coach's role should be to support a person in the development of new skills and capacities to be successful.

I think of a coach as responsible for working with others primarily on the development of technical skills and increasing knowledge of the material, though certainly coaches need to attend to the emotional needs of those they assist. Good listening skills are essential. A critical part of the job is to identify and point out mentees' strengths so that that they can use them to greater advantage and have confidence in their job and performance. While at times

I use the words "coach" and "mentor" synonymously in this book, coaching could be thought of in a more limited way as one aspect of the mentor's role.

A common form of coaching used in American schools is Cognitive Coaching, as described by Costa and Garmston (2002). This approach assumes that behaviors change after beliefs evolve. The emphasis therefore is on reflection and changing one's perceptions as a prerequisite to changing actions. Whether belief precedes action, or at other times it is the reverse, with changes in behavior causing changes in thinking, the goal of Cognitive Coaching is to produce self-directed educators with the cognitive capacity for excellent performance individually and as a part of the school community (Costa and Garmston 2002, 16). That is a worthy mission, and the coaching examples provided in this book do, in fact, illustrate this process of self-reflection encouraged by a mentor–coach, as the authors prescribe.

Jim Knight uses the term "instructional coaching," which is a role aptly suited to the mentor model presented in this text. As he puts it, "A good coach is an excellent teacher and is kind-hearted, respectful, patient, compassionate, and honest" (Knight 2007, 15). This person has high expectations and gives both positive and honest feedback to the partner teacher. We have trained many exemplary instructional coaches who work in partnerships to build on colleagues' strengths, and help each person reach for excellence.

What Do Mentors and Coaches Do?

What mentors can do to support teachers depends on how their role is structured. The ideal, in my way of thinking, is to assign a full-time mentor within one school to work with a small group of teachers. Full-time mentors, trained and released from teaching for two or more years, have time to learn how to effectively perform their roles, and focus on helping their colleagues attain their professional goals. Teachers who mentor part time feel stretched by leaving their own classrooms to assist others. Often, two part-time assignments become much more than a full-time job as they prepare lessons for substitutes to use with their students and, at the same time, contemplate and oversee the next steps for each of their mentees.

Selecting as a mentor a highly respected and effective teacher from within a school's faculty, rather than bringing in someone unfamiliar with the school, can speed up the process of getting to know the mentees and creating close working relationships. Mentors who work with a group of teachers at one school only, rather than traveling across a district to various schools, have more time and opportunities to plan with teachers and answer their questions in spontaneous meetings and hallway conversations, as well as during their regularly scheduled sessions for observing, debriefing, and planning.

Most importantly, the number of teachers assigned to a mentor in one school affects the results. Five to eight teachers form a large enough cohort to share ideas, stimulate dialogue, and learn from each other in a formal structure such as a study group, and informally, as they attend observations or workshops together. Groups larger than eight make it difficult for the mentor to schedule enough classroom visits and debriefing sessions with every teacher weekly. Consistently having weekly in-classroom observations and out-of-classroom meetings keeps the momentum for change on track.

This small ratio of mentor to a group of teachers is expensive and requires a substantial investment of a school's budget and/or a district's resources. The results are more striking, however, when the teachers are given this level of support to make substantial changes in their practice. The mentor can work directly with each of five to eight teachers for two to three hours every week. At times, the work they do together happens in the classroom with students present. At other times, it occurs while they are watching exemplary teachers at other schools, during workshops they attend jointly, or in meeting rooms where the teachers and the mentor do their planning. Full-time mentoring like this, with a manageable ratio of mentor to mentees, is intense and rare. It is this complete dedication of a mentor to a group of eager teachers that advances their learning far more than when the ratio of teachers to coach is closer to 15 or 20 to one and contact is far less frequent.

Coaching is a vital part of the mentor's role, but coaching good, competent teachers who have been in the profession for years is very different from coaching potential teachers working on their credentials or those still in the probationary phase of their careers. Especially with teachers with more years of experience than themselves, mentors cannot expect to walk into rooms and be well received as a coach if they simply tell their colleagues what to do and what not to do. The mentors, instead, must provide honest feedback on a lesson without making a judgment or giving specific directions about what needs to change. The mentor's aim should be to help partner teachers analyze their own teaching. Throughout the school year, mentors conduct regular cycles of observation–debriefing–planning with each person, giving each an opportunity to practice self-reflection and plan the next steps to improve instruction.

The content of what good instructors need to learn is also far different from what inexperienced teachers need. Mentors of new teachers show them ways to manage student behavior, organize the classroom, select curriculum, and structure lessons from beginning to end. In contrast, mentors of experienced and competent educators focus on helping them understand the subjects they teach in greater depth. They assist them by identifying new methods to differentiate instruction so that they can present the same concepts and skills to all the children, while also varying the complexity of the materials and the pacing of the work so that each child will have a better chance of succeeding. Mentors guide their high-performing mentees in teaching self-management skills to students so that their pupils can become even more responsible for their own learning and behavior. Developing formative assessments, perfecting questioning techniques, tightening lessons so that they are more coherent and focused, finding a variety of ways to introduce various models students can use to approach their assignments, differentiating instruction to fit each child—these are all common challenges addressed by mentors as they assist experienced and skillful teachers to improve.

Mentors of experienced teachers also perform a variety of other tasks. They may videotape lessons to give their partner teachers feedback. They help them recognize their teaching strengths and set professional goals. Mentor and mentee regularly conduct an observation–debrief–plan cycle and assess student progress. They act as coaches and offer demonstration lessons. Mentors also create a sense of community and opportunities for professional dialogue among the participating teachers.

Videotaping Instruction

Videotaping has proved to be a highly effective tool to assist teachers employing new approaches in the classroom. Mentors videotape each of their partner teachers conducting a lesson at the start and end of each school year, and sometimes with more frequency. The mentor and teacher plan the first lesson, review the tape immediately after the lesson, and deconstruct what they see to hypothesize what to try next. They examine the students' performance during the lesson. Who is learning? How much of the content do the children understand? Where in the lesson do students make errors and why? What could the teacher try next to move each pupil to a higher level? At the end of the school year, mentor and mentee review early and recent videos to compare how the teaching has changed and whether the students responded more positively during the latter sessions.

As you can imagine, some teachers can feel intimidated by the thought of being videotaped. It takes time to get used to seeing oneself on camera. Yet most find the exercise so valuable that they put aside their initial discomfort and ask their mentors to videotape them more than twice during the year to identify the small elements of change taking place over time. Some mentors also audiotape students' discussions to capture the quality of thinking and the extent of participation happening in small groups.

Setting a Goal

Expanding the teacher's repertoire of pedagogical techniques so that he or she can be more effective in reaching each child is a primary aim of a comprehensive learning program. Selecting a content focus will determine the teaching methods teachers choose to pursue. The content and the pedagogy used to teach it are interconnected. The next steps in goal-setting then involve spelling out the teaching methods or skills he or she will learn, describing how the teaching will look as a consequence, listing the training to attend, specifying academic goals the students will reach, and identifying existing assessments or developing new ones to be used to measure student learning. The teacher's goals should include a detailed projection of how professional development will play out over the year and a prediction of the effects of changes in practice on the students. Partner teachers and mentors regularly review signs of progress toward the teaching goals and the expected student outcomes. They may make frequent mid-course corrections in the teaching to achieve the goals they have set.

Observing–Debriefing–Planning

The observation–debrief–plan cycle used by mentors accomplishes several purposes. When mentors watch their mentees instruct children, teaching becomes a public act shared with others so that the adults can learn how to improve teaching together. Mentors can collect data requested by the mentee and offer appropriate feedback immediately or in later private conversations. The debrief part of the cycle is a time when mentors encourage self-reflection in their partners by asking open-ended questions about the lesson and its effects on the students. The mentee identifies the strengths of instruction that he or she wants to repeat and preserve, considers what students understood and what failed to help the students, and then contemplates how to alter or refine the teaching to have greater effect on the children's learning. The planning part of the cycle involves the mentee specifying the next steps to take to practice or try new approaches.

Coaching in the Classroom

Intensive coaching two or more hours weekly helps teachers keep focused and embeds their learning into their day-to-day patterns of teaching. Teachers decide the teaching method they will practice. A teacher may want the mentor to give feedback on how well he or she articulated the purpose of the lesson, whether the individual feedback given to students was specific and on target to meet their needs, or if the "turn-and-talk" activity for students was productive. The teachers then determine the kind of data they want the mentor to collect. These data may include information such as what children say and do while working in small groups, or which students are doing the talking in class and how they articulate their thoughts, or when and how the teacher responded to an impromptu comment from a student and built on it for future instruction. During a lesson, coaching may require only a brief whisper in the ear of the teacher. Sometimes a simple hand signal reminds the presenter to try a specific technique. More in-depth coaching occurs when the mentor raises questions after the lesson and as the partners examine the data collected during the observation.

One fruitful example of coaching emerged early in one school year after a group of mentees observed a cadre of exceptional teachers. Seeing the amount of student interaction and student work taking place in that other school, they asked their mentor to collect data on the amount of instructional time spent in their own classrooms on teacher talk, student talk, and student work. Results showed that 75 to 90 percent of each lesson was taken up by the teachers talking. They did almost all the work, while students sat silent. Disheartened by these results, they agreed to set a goal of cutting down on the time spent giving directions, repeating steps, and telling children what and how to do short assignments. They changed roles and started asking students to talk about their thinking, to explain how they did their work, and to model their individual ways of finding solutions or interpreting text for others in the class. The kids blossomed as they actively engaged in solving problems and applying the knowledge they were learning.

Box 5.1   Pause & Reflect

How has a coach helped you in your practice? How would you structure a coaching program at your school or district to promote continuous improvement in teaching? If you have a coaching program, what would you do to make it even more effective?

Demonstrating Teaching Methods

At the partner teacher's request, mentors also demonstrate how to use an approach. The mentee observes and acts as the data collector. They do this as colleagues who are learning together, and when they debrief the lesson, they talk about what went well and what rough edges need to be smoothed.

One teacher noticed how artfully her mentor would demonstrate a next step to take without directly telling her what she should be doing and how to do it. The mentee found this more inviting way of coaching worked well for her, both for her own learning and as she began to assist others at her school. She describes how her own coaching went.

> It's a serious, trusting relationship. I was coaching in math and trying to model my mentor. I went into a room and we set up the equation together. I watched the teacher tell the children how to solve it. I'm thinking, "You're not supposed to tell them how to solve it." I thought, "How do I do this?" So, I said, "You know what? I'm very excited and I have this new idea. I'd love to teach math in your room for one day." So, I went in and modeled how to do the problem. Afterwards, she said to me, "Well, you didn't tell them how to do the problem and solve it, but they did!" Some of the kids that day made big "Ah ha"s! There were kids counting by nickels sitting next to somebody doing tallies who realized they could count these in a different way. They could count by fives. Then it was great seeing them circling and saying, "Oh, that's a five. That's a five." She could see that they make more "ah ha"s by not being told what tools they must use to solve the problem. Let them use what they're comfortable with.

Facilitating Study Groups

Mentoring creates a weekly dialogue about teaching and learning between the individual teacher and his or her mentor. Study groups involving the mentor and a cluster of teachers expand the conversation. The groups give teachers a way to work together and learn from each other within their own school settings. The team of teachers typically investigates questions of practice that interest them. They may watch videos of teaching and identify the elements that are or are not working. Some read professional texts, raise questions, try out the ideas, and report back the results of implementation. Others conduct action research in which they test teaching tactics new to them and devise ways to gauge the effects on students. Lesson Study groups construct a lesson together, test it out in classrooms, and then revise their plan as needed. Another common practice is also gathering and analyzing data on student learning and considering in what direction the data suggest they should move. Mentors help plan and facilitate the agendas for the group meetings based upon the interests of the participating teachers.

An Example of the Complexities of Mentoring

Some of the challenges to performing the mentor role are illustrated by the case of a mentor who had 25 years' prior teaching experience. Her difficult, albeit common task in the Art of Teaching, was to mentor a group of fellows who had taught from 4 to 23 years. Each had different needs based on their professional experiences, their strengths, and the grade levels to which they were assigned, ranging from kindergarten through fifth grade.

What made her task more difficult were across-the-board reassignments of most of her fellows. A kindergarten teacher chose reading as her area of focus for both years of the fellowship, as did the first- and second-grade teachers. However, the first-grade teacher was moved to grade two in her second year of the fellowship and the second-grade teacher was asked to take a first- and second-grade combination class, a challenge to both them and their mentor because they needed to address slightly different reading goals in year two. Similarly, the third-grade instructor who picked writing as her subject the first year, changed to reading in year two when given a first-grade class. The fourth-grade and fifth-grade teachers picked math and stayed with that subject even though the fifth-grade teacher moved to a first-grade class in her last year of the program. Flexibility and adaptability to change were required by all.

A critical component of this mentor's success was her ability to develop trust with each of her mentees. She respected and supported them. They, in turn, set aside all reticence and became fully engaged in their training. All succeeded in making remarkable improvements in both their teaching and the performance of their students. This mentor had the training she needed to know how to build and maintain trust with colleagues, as well as to deal with the complexities of her job and support her partnering teachers so that they could attain their professional goals.

Training of Mentors and Coaches

Selecting mentors or coaches from among the best teachers at a school is only a beginning. No matter how capable they are in teaching young people, they are not necessarily naturals who have all the skills useful when working with other adults. Some chosen as mentors have a head start if they already work well with other adults and are generally positive and encouraging individuals. In addition to these interpersonal skills, most new mentors will need to learn techniques for how to work effectively to support colleagues who are struggling to implement new practices.

Coaching experienced and capable teachers is an unusual role and one for which the coach or mentor needs training in different methods of facilitating the learning of another adult, rather than directing that person. Choosing the best strategies to help others evaluate their teaching performance and decide what to alter is an essential part of the mentor's job. Mentors working with experienced teachers learn how to establish a confidential and mutually respectful relationship, how to help them set goals for improvements in both the teaching and student learning, and how to select or design assessments to collect evidence of the effects of the teaching on students. Most importantly, mentors must position themselves as learners alongside the teachers as they explore together a variety of ways to elevate teaching to a much higher level.

Carrie Valentine, a former math resource teacher for Madison Metropolitan School District and an instructional coach at Lincoln Elementary School in Madison, Wisconsin, has told us how she learned to perfect her own work and then discussed her thoughts on what others need as they study their teaching. To improve her own instruction, Carrie watched other teachers who were reflective and challenged her thinking, observed teachers of students younger than those in her classes because she was amazed by what those students could do, completed a Master of Arts degree in mathematics education, and did a lot of reading about research and teaching methods. Carrie mentioned how important it is for teachers to have support from university faculty to keep up to date on research, plus the support of other more knowledgeable teachers around them. About coaching, she pointed out that these individuals need to be good at reflective practice, but that that is not enough. They need to be thoroughly grounded in the content. "Teachers may have trouble at first, talking about what they and the kids know. Because I had studied math education for so long, I could address on the spot an issue that arose for a teacher." She added:

> I have always learned the most by listening and thinking about what kids do and say in response to the problems I give them and the questions I ask. My goal in professional development is to help teachers learn to do the same. If no one says "I learn by listening to my kids," then I know we have work to do. At another level, I also have learned what is effective in professional development by listening and thinking about what teachers do and say in response to what I ask them to do and the questions I ask. So, it's really all the same. Learning is about listening and trying to understand what is being communicated. I think that's true for everyone and for all subjects.

Mentors in the Art of Teaching receive training throughout their two-year assignments. Training begins in late spring with new mentors shadowing experienced mentors on the job. They spend a day following their hosts into classes and planning meetings. They watch an observe–debrief–plan cycle.

With the mentor, they review teachers' goals and the assessments used to measure students' progress. Together, they may view classroom videos from the start and end of the current school year, comparing their impressions of how the teaching changed. They go over the mechanics of the job, such as scheduling substitutes, ordering supplies, paying for expenses, and preparing reports. They talk about the nuances of working with the principal, including agreeing upon the kinds of information that can be discussed openly versus confidences that must be strictly maintained to sustain the trust of the partner teachers. The experienced mentor describes how the participants are encouraged to share the benefits of the Art of Teaching fellowship with other teachers at the school, piquing others' interest and potentially spreading the effects of the program. Shadowing gives new mentors a feel for the range of tasks they will need to perform and a sense of the variety in the roles they need to play in their interactions with the teachers and principals.

Over the summer and early fall, new mentors come together for several days of training conducted by consultants and staff from the Cotsen Foundation. They investigate artful teaching by viewing videos of exemplary teachers and discussing elements of excellence seen in the lessons. Mentors learn about methods for promoting self-reflection by asking questions such as, "How do you think the lesson went? Why?" and "What might you see in your class if you . . . ?" Developing trust and maintaining confidentiality about the partner teacher's professional growth are stressed. They then examine the value of tasks that launch the year, including videotaping lessons, attending the foundation's annual conference, and observing artful teachers at other schools. Mentors devise ways to use the information and inspiration stemming from these start-up activities to help their mentees formulate goals for growth that year.

Mentors also need guidelines to help them construct and facilitate monthly inquiry or study group meetings. During training, mentors look at examples and generate their own ideas on topics, research questions, and tasks participating teachers may choose to explore with each other. The point of monthly meetings is to give mentees time to engage in scholarly discussion about subject-matter content, teaching methods, and student learning. Mentor training centers on ways to guide the group conversations into a deeper and richer exploration of content in subsequent meetings.

All mentors meet monthly during the school year to continue their training and to problem-solve together. Most of these meetings are designed and facilitated by pairs composed of one novice and one experienced mentor, giving each practice in running meetings and leading groups. On occasion, Art of Teaching alumni attend as guest speakers or small-group leaders, bringing additional expertise to the discussions.

Finally, all mentors are assigned a liaison from the Cotsen Foundation whose job it is to make sure that the mentor has the tools, resources, and support he or she needs to perform the job. Mentors themselves benefit from having a mentor, or at least a supportive advocate, as they pursue their line of work.

Summary

In-classroom support and coaching are the keys to teachers changing their practice and implementing new approaches. Successful mentors establish trusting relationships with mentees, build upon the strengths of individuals, and perform a variety of tasks to help them. Because of the complexity and demands of the mentor's role, even excellent teachers will need some targeted training to perform more effectively. Training should include ways to establish a trusting partnership with teachers, help them get a vision of how to build upon their strengths, to observe–debrief–plan with mentees, encourage self-reflection, coach in the classroom, and offer appropriate feedback.

Additional Resources

For those seeking further guidance on how to structure the role of a mentor or coach, and those who want to organize an effective training program for these individuals, there are many excellent references which provide lots of detail and many tools. Jim Knight paints a vivid picture of instructional coaching in his book, *Instructional Coaching: A Partnership Approach to Improving Instruction* (2007). The cognitive coaching model is presented in depth by Costa and Garmston in *Cognitive Coaching: A Foundation for Renaissance Schools* (2002). In *The Art of Coaching: Effective Strategies for School Transformation* (2013) and *The Art of Coaching Teams: Building Resilient Communities that Transform Schools* (2016), Elena Aguilar describes the foundations for coaches which help them affect whole schools and she delineates the types of professional development they need to fulfill their critical role.

References

Aguilar, Elena. 2013. *The Art of Coaching: Effective Strategies for School Transformation*. San Francisco, CA: Jossey-Bass.

Aguilar, Elena. 2016. *The Art of Coaching Teams: Building Resilient Communities that Transform Schools*. San Francisco, CA: Jossey-Bass.

Bush, Robert N. 1984. *Effective Staff Developments in Making Our Schools More Effective: Proceedings of Three State Conferences.* San Francisco, CA: Far West Laboratories, 223–232.

Costa, Arthur L., and Robert J. Garmston. 2002. *Cognitive Coaching: A Foundation for Renaissance Schools.* Norwood, MA: Christopher-Gordon.

Knight, Jim. 2007. *Instructional Coaching: A Partnership Approach to Improving Instruction.* Thousand Oaks, CA: Corwin Press.

Yoon, Kwan. S., Teresa Duncan, Silvia Wen-Yu Lee, Beth Scarloss, and Kathy L. Shapley. 2007. "Reviewing the Evidence on How Teacher Professional Development Affects Student Achievement," *Issues & Answers Report*, REL 2007–No.033. Washington, D.C.: U.S. Department of Education, Institute of Education Sciences, National Center for Education Evaluation and Regional Assistance, Regional Educational Laboratory Southwest. Retrieved November 4, 2017 from http://ies.ed.gov/ncee/edlabs.

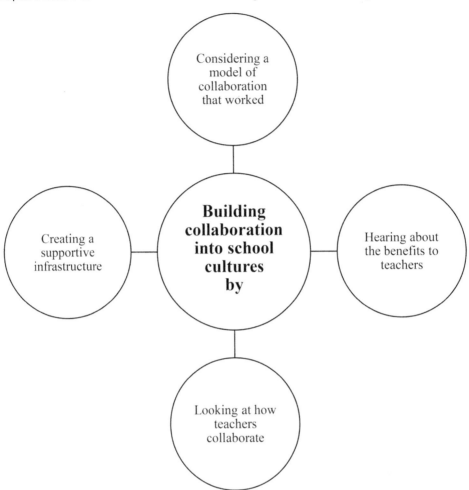

6

Collaborate with Colleagues and Make Teaching Public

People don't progress unless they leave their classrooms and meet with each other.
(Kristin Gibson, Professional Development Facilitator for Arkansas,
Teachers Development Group)

Each of the components of a comprehensive professional development program combines to get greater results, and one of the most important of these is teacher collaboration. Sharing knowledge and working together for a common goal are present in standout schools that are making a difference for student learning (Garmston and Wellman 1999, 13). Research reinforces the observation that schools characterized by high levels of teacher collaboration achieve higher levels of student achievement than schools where teachers work in isolation (Blank, de las Alas, and Smith 2008).

A Model of Collaboration that Worked

The concept of reaching out to learn from colleagues is not new. Decades ago the Cleveland Humanities Magnet High School in Los Angeles Unified School District operated a popular program of thematic, interdisciplinary, writing-based instruction for students from a variety of neighborhoods in that sprawling city. The Magnet school coordinator, Neil Anstead, along with a few of his teachers who had prior experience teaching in lower-income neighborhoods, were convinced that this approach, which was both engaging and challenging, would have the same successful results regardless of the economic, social, and educational backgrounds of the students being taught. Joining forces with the nonprofit Los Angeles Education Partnership, they set about opening their rooms for observations and consultation with visiting teachers about ways to implement these methods. They trained dozens of teams of high school teachers of English, history, economics, philosophy, and art. These teams, in turn, changed the academic lives of their students. Thousands of teenagers previously adrift in their high schools became successful graduates and matriculated to college. The talented teachers at the Cleveland Humanities Magnet became a seedbed for growth in the 1980s and 1990s, contributing to a transformation of high school instruction in pockets of this large, urban area for more than 20 years. The results of their work can still be seen in L.A. schools that participated in what was called the "Humanitas" program. Other schools and districts across the country have looked to this model of instruction as a guide for their own teaching. The faculty at Cleveland Magnet School were particularly persuasive because they were performing in their own classrooms and could use their own teaching as models and guides for potential improvement.

I believe that the attraction of teachers to Humanitas and its staying power over more than two decades was due in large part to the fact that teachers worked together to share their content knowledge, shape curriculum, assess their students, solve problems, and support each other in teams committed to greater student success. The professional relationships with each other and the personal commitments to the young people they taught made teaching even more meaningful. The frequent debates about what to teach, how to present it, and ways to know if students understand the content and have developed the skills of oral argumentation and persuasive writing across subject matter transformed teaching into an intellectual profession founded on reflection, nonstop learning, and self-improvement. Having observed high school teachers like this achieve exceptional teaching and dramatic results for their students made me wonder what elementary school instructors could accomplish when given the opportunity to work together to continuously refine what and how they taught.

The Benefits of Collaboration

Collaboration contributes to improving the quality of teaching. Constantly adjusting and refining the details of instruction based on student learning outcomes is best accomplished by a team of committed educators. Citing the international TIMSS research about features of mathematics instruction that predict student learning, Stigler and Hiebert (2009) point out that U.S.

students do less well than students of many other countries because their teachers have little access to models demonstrating ways to teach as well as inadequate curricular support. To enhance teaching performance, they call for relentless attention to student learning goals, closer examination of student work, and greater analysis of teaching and learning as cause and effect. The authors urge that structures be put in place so that teachers have more opportunities to plan, practice, observe, and share with each other (Stigler and Hiebert 2009, 144). Collaboration, in other words, is a cornerstone for growth in both teaching and student achievement.

Among the best reasons for teachers to collaborate on joint projects is to have wider input into selecting or developing more demanding instructional materials. Sharing with a diverse group of educators gives the individuals access to a wider pool of practical knowledge and creative ideas than each would have working alone or only in grade-level teams. Problem-solving and learning new material can be more fruitful with another's help. Tackling time-consuming or challenging tasks as a team often seems less difficult as members encourage each other to persist in their efforts. Teachers can also offer mutual support when they take the risk of using new methods, and experience the awkwardness and occasional failure that come with trying something different.

Both teachers and their students want to be assured that the children are capable of higher levels of understanding and achievement. Teachers discover unexpected possibilities for their pupils after watching students reach higher goals in the classes of masterful instructors. They can be inspired to expand their instructional tool kits and strive to heighten their effectiveness with their own pupils because of what other teachers have made public and shared with them.

Most elementary schools are structured in ways which isolate teachers. Such structures work against the kind of ongoing collaboration needed for dramatic and steady improvement. Dr. Brett Geithman, former principal of Juan Bautista Alvarado Elementary School in Long Beach, described how making teaching public and giving teachers opportunities to learn together addressed this issue of isolation. He talked about the benefits to his school from increased collaboration:

Hosting observations for others, visiting other school sites within or outside of their district, collaborating with teachers across schools and districts, and attending professional development workshops together— through these experiences, teachers genuinely collaborated and reflected with fellow teachers, resulting in better instruction and, ultimately, student achievement. This work also evolved into building a cadre of site leaders, first with the mentor and participating teachers, and then expanding across the campus due to their work. I can say confidently that the depth of understanding in best practice, along with the student successes seen year after year, are in large part due to the leadership and collaboration fostered at our site. The idea that all teachers are continuously growing and reflecting is evident in all classrooms at my school.

Cindy Wechsung, a fourth-grade teacher at Alvarado, succinctly described the change at the school: "This is a Helen Keller story. 'Alone we can do so little. Together we can do so much.'"

Collaborative structures such as those put in place at Alvarado—those that involve analysis of practice in light of student results and frequent observation of other teachers—offer another benefit. They provide benchmarks against which teachers can evaluate their own practices. They can compare what they do with the methods used by others and set their aims on steady improvement toward higher standards of performance.

The changes in tone at a collaborative school, in which educators view themselves as a community of professionals, are visible and important. A different type of conversation takes place during meetings and even in the teachers' lounge. Another instructor elaborated on the altered environment: "Teachers are more aware of their teaching practice and of the need to focus on learning. Conversations are deeper and focus more often on pedagogy. There is a tone of professional pride that was not there before."

The shift she describes is toward more talk about teaching practices that are getting results with kids. There is more conversation about professional readings, research, or courses taken and what was learned. Teachers devote more time to reflecting upon what they do and how their actions and words affect children. The entire school benefits when the responsibility for school improvement and student learning is more broadly distributed.

Cathy Lien wrote at length in a newsletter article about the excitement teachers at her school, Heideman Elementary in Tustin, had for observing great teaching in other districts. Their enthusiasm affected the conversation of their entire faculty, and as a result, they all began working together to change the school's approach to professional development.

Word started getting out. My colleagues at Heideman wanted to know more about Reader's Workshop and CGI Math. Spearheaded by our mentor and modeled after a popular practice at Weaver Elementary, "Iron Sharpens Iron" days, as we call them, were created. Now all teachers at Heideman would have the opportunity to enter into other teachers classrooms to observe the already wonderful things going on at our site. This is what teachers had wanted to do for years and now it was happening. I'm proud to report that at our last "Iron Sharpens Iron" day, nearly 100 percent of our staff participated.

When teachers share their knowledge about practices that work for them, they begin to establish a common understanding of what is effective and what is not. This common understanding can strengthen the profession overall. Scholarship—investigating teaching and its effects on students—changes the profession from one of isolation and dependence on one's own training and ideas to a communal enterprise. A community of thinkers provides the teachers with knowledge resources far more expansive and trustworthy than is usually available to educators.

Ongoing collaborative learning, focused on subjects of value to the participants, changes individual teachers, schools, and school systems. Examples of what principals and superintendents have done to promote continuous professional growth and collaborative learning are offered in the next chapter.

How Teachers Collaborate

Collaboration takes many forms. Coaching, demonstration lessons, and lab classes are examples described in some detail in previous chapters. Joining with a small group of colleagues to investigate teaching is another approach. A few schools encourage groups of teachers to conduct action research, in which they test a teaching approach new to them and devise ways to gauge the effects on students. In study groups or inquiry meetings, teams wrestle with "essential questions" of practice or conduct practical research on how their teaching methods work with pupils. Together, teachers plan curricular units, select appropriate instructional materials to get better results, and identify or create assessments to measure changes in student understanding of material.

Lesson Study (Hurd and Lewis 2011) is a formal structure for teacher research that can contribute to the collective refinement of instructional plans and greater student learning. A common form of teacher collaboration in Japan, it allows faculties to share tested lessons with educators across the country. This process gives teams of teachers a significant role in shaping effective instruction. The aim is to improve student learning and understanding. The focus is on finding how students respond to instruction, and identifying changes in lessons which will strengthen student comprehension and skill. The practice is a joint venture among teachers within a school done over several months. Teachers develop a lesson together. One of them teaches it while the others observe and take notes. In discussions afterwards, they identify the strengths and weaknesses in the instruction and revise the lesson plan. Another teacher demonstrates the new lesson as the others watch. The cycle is repeated until an effective lesson is shaped by the team. They then share their research results with others through demonstration lessons and publications. Participating teachers contribute to the knowledge base of the profession, while they themselves learn what methods work best with students.

Another example of a study group in the Encinitas Union School District in the northern San Diego County in California demonstrates how powerful and motivating collaborative professional learning can be. The group started with a grant for 12 K-6 teachers to study mathematics instruction, and eventually the group grew to 20 members. They met monthly to watch video clips along with Professor Vicki Jacobs from San Diego State University who facilitated the teachers' conversations. Before the study group meeting, members were sometimes given the problem to be discussed so that they could try it out with their own classes in advance. This gave them all a common starting point for the 85-minute exchange they would have. Each teacher prepared and then chose one clip or a sample of student work to share with the group. The clip shows the teacher presenting the problem, a student working on solving it, and the two of them talking about the child's thinking. Through these interviews, the teachers learned how the children understood the mathematics. Together they generated ideas on how to build upon and extend that thinking. By making teaching public in the video clips, the members could compare their own work with that of peers, pose a range of hypotheses about children's choices and thoughts, share ideas on next steps in instruction, and support each other with positive feedback. Because they had established a respectful and trusting relationship over time, they could also act as a "critical friend" with their colleagues, raising questions and giving suggestions about teaching techniques to advance the practice of everyone in the study group. The core dozen members of the group chose to continue for 12 more years after the grant concluded, facilitating their own conversations and learning from each other.

Meghan Ling, a group member from start to finish, pointed out how important what she called "progressive leadership" is to the formation and survival of vital study groups such as this.

> Teachers need time to talk with each other and reflect. They need the freshest research on teaching and learning. Teaching is the best profession in the world, but it's a process. You need to give yourself a lot of time to perfect your craft and find out who you are. Every year, one child will throw you a curve. You have to think again. It's always changing. It's always new. You have to keep learning at a deeper level and then put it into practice.

Principals and district administrators who understand the value of providing sustained time over several years for educators to work together, can make it possible for teachers to continuously improve and aim for excellence in their instruction. Ms. Ling and other members of her study group wholeheartedly embraced working with colleagues, and went on to become leaders of professional learning inside their own district and in other school systems as well.

Box 6.1   Pause & Reflect

What are some ways school faculties could build even more shared knowledge about practices that improve student learning?

Creating a Supportive Infrastructure

What else needs to be done to make teaching public, and foster collaboration? The first step is to allocate more time and opportunities for teachers to talk with each other about their teaching. According to a MetLife Survey of the American Teacher (2010), most teachers reported that they were given some sort of structured collaboration time, but fewer than one-third of them and their principals said that time was used to observe each other and give feedback.

Many schools now "bank" time by lengthening the minutes in each school day and then use the chunks of time saved for weekly staff meetings of an hour or more when students come to school later or leave early. Principals then design these staff meetings specifically to involve faculty in conversations about teaching and learning, while routine notices and transmission of more general information are handled mostly through websites and emails. The faculty may look at student benchmark results or standardized test data to analyze results. They may examine student work in small groups to identify strengths and weaknesses in order to plan additions or changes to instruction. Teachers often meet by grade levels or in department groups to share breakthrough lessons. Some principals ask teachers at the school to present examples of new practices that are achieving positive effects.

Many schools have set up Professional Learning Communities (PLCs) following the guidelines of Richard and Roberta DuFour, and their co-authors (2016). The focus of the learning community is on working together to achieve learning for all participants, creating structures to promote a collaborative culture, and attending to results in terms of student achievement. As Richard DuFour explains, questions such as, "What do we want each student to learn and how will we know when the student has learned it?" and "How will we respond when a student experiences difficulty in learning?" should drive the faculty conversation and collaborative work (DuFour 2004, 6).

To promote continuous improvement in teaching, and increase student learning as a consequence, schools and districts need to establish an infrastructure for collaborative learning. Teacher leaders can assist in initiating and managing those structures, whether they be Lesson Study, Communities of Practice, a Professional Learning Community, or teachers as researchers. Where there are few experienced teacher leaders, principals can step in to introduce these structures and then work closely with the faculty to nurture the future teacher leaders who will guide the work. The commitment to this process will need to be long term. It will take time for collaboration to become a habit and part of the culture of the school. If the work teachers share is of their choice and of value to their success with students, collaboration becomes a habit which teachers will cherish and want to continue.

A note of caution: In my years of experience working with educators, I have found that collaborative work should be kept private so that teachers can be more candid in sharing their setbacks as well as their positive outcomes. Teachers' efforts to improve with the help of others should not be linked to formal teacher evaluations tied to job performance. Being public about teaching, and breaking down the isolation, will be more likely to spread when educators feel safe to reveal their successes, as well as those things which work less well, so that all may learn from each person's experience. Creating a climate of safety and trust is paramount.

Teachers also need to be clear about the goals of the collaborative effort, and even direct these ventures. So many redesigns of schools run afoul due to faulty implementation. Vague or confusing goals easily derail reforms. It helps if teacher leaders, or the entire faculty, are trained in how to implement collaboration with fidelity, how to set norms and maintain them, and how to run meetings efficiently while preserving a respectful climate.

Summary

Collaboration has the power to change the teaching profession into an energizing and dynamic career-long experience of perfecting one's craft with colleagues in a community of scholarship.

- ◆ By working together teachers improve the quality of teaching, get diverse ideas, and share the workload when developing curriculum and methods.
- ◆ There are many formats for collaborative work, including mentoring, observing instruction, participating in lab classes, engaging in study group work, and Lesson Study.
- ◆ Schools and districts need to establish an infrastructure which provides time to work together, helps teachers set specific goals, and offers some training in facilitating group work.

References

Blank, Rolf K., Nina de las Alas, and Carlise Smith. 2008. *Does Teacher Professional Development Have Effects on Teaching and Learning? Analysis of Evaluation Findings from Programs for Mathematics and Science Teachers in 14 States.* Retrieved November 4, 2017 from http://www.ccsso.org/documents/2008/does_teacher_professional_development_2008.pdf.

DuFour, Richard. 2004. "What Is a Professional Learning Community?" *Educational Leadership: Journal of the Department of Supervision and Curriculum Development* 61(8): 6–11.

DuFour, Richard, Rebecca DuFour, Robert Eaker, Thomas Many, and Mike Mattos. 2016. *Learning by Doing: A Handbook for Professional Learning Communities at Work.* Bloomington, IN: Solution Tree Press.

Garmston, Robert J. and Bruce Wellman. 1999. *The Adaptive School: A Sourcebook for Developing Collaborative Groups.* Norwood, MA: Christopher-Gordon.

Hurd, Jacqueline, and Catherine Lewis. 2011. *Lesson Study Step by Step: How Teacher Learning Communities Improve Instruction.* Portsmouth, NH: Heinemann.

MetLife. 2010. *Met Life Survey of the American Teacher: Collaborating for Student Success.* Retrieved November 4, 2017 from https://eric.ed.gov/?q=met+life+survey+of+the+American+teacher%3A+collaborating+for+success/.

Stigler, James, and James Hiebert. 2009. *The Teaching Gap: Best Ideas from the World's Teachers for Improving Education in the Classroom.* New York: Free Press.

7

Key Roles of School and District Leaders

School and district leadership is essential if a comprehensive professional development program is to be implemented. Superintendents, assistant superintendents for curriculum and instruction, other district administrators supporting teaching, and principals, all play roles in setting the advancement of teaching and learning as a priority. They have significant control over the resources needed to put a sophisticated professional learning plan in place. They can promote and support practices which lead to the continuous improvement of teaching.

An elementary school principal's job is particularly difficult because it includes so many different pieces. The principal oversees the budgets and purchasing, the facilities and maintenance, school safety concerns, human resources and performance reviews, some student discipline, direct contact with parents and guardians, plus community relations and fundraising. On top of that, the principal is responsible for the quality of teaching and learning, ongoing professional development at the school level, testing and assessment, and compliance with pertinent laws and regulations. Special education concerns are especially demanding of the principal's time and vigilance. Despite these competing agendas, a good number of principals have come to appreciate the importance of providing more effective ways to help teachers elevate their craftsmanship and improve student achievement.

More principals and their district administrators must implement a more focused and comprehensive professional development. In determining what type of programs best fit their teachers' needs and aspirations, planners and leaders of professional development within the system should utilize an inquiry approach like the one teachers have discovered to be important to use with their students. They will guide rather than direct people through learning experiences. Administrators may need to refine their listening and questioning skills to draw out and understand the best thinking of teachers.

When continuous improvement of teaching and learning are the goals, administrators are more likely to succeed when they build upon the strengths of their most talented teachers. Using them as workshop leaders, facilitators, or mentors will draw the other faculty members in to participate. They will welcome having a mentor to support their growth, rather than seeing coaching as an activity designed to repair inadequacies. As more teachers become involved, they are more likely to enhance their individual instruction when they are offered a range of options including workshops, demonstration lessons, coaching situations, lab classes, study groups, cross-school networks, and other components of professional development that address specific pedagogical methods and content areas.

Three Successful Examples

Two schools and one district involved in the Art of Teaching illustrate how school and district leaders have strengthened teaching and student learning throughout their schools and districts.

A Complete Transformation

I first visited Weaver Elementary in the solidly middle-class community of Los Alamitos with my colleague, Barbara Golding, from the Cotsen Foundation. A principal in a nearby district told us that the math instruction at Weaver was superior. We went somewhat reluctantly because our primary mission was not to find different pedagogical approaches. We hoped to find one or two exemplary teachers who could serve as models for others in the Art of Teaching fellowship. Instead, we were astonished to discover great teaching going on in class after class. Weaver was a goldmine for us. We had found a treasure trove of exciting teaching to which we could send our fellows to observe and learn from gifted teachers whose students tackled math and all other subjects with vigor.

Erin Kominsky, who was the principal at that time, explained to us how Weaver changed from a dormant facility to a school with long waiting lists of parents applying for their children to attend. The Board of Education decided to redraw the boundaries and open the site on a year-round calendar. Ms. Kominsky was hired and she hand-picked the staff for innovation, passion, and commitment. She selected an educator experienced in Cognitively Guided Instruction to be the school's trainer and coach in mathematics, as well as one of the faculty. Where the true work came into play was in the professional learning meetings they conducted each week where the conversation focused on how students learn. They modeled "Kaizen," or continuous improvement, and went on to explore innovative teaching in reading, writing, and Socratic seminar. Weaver has gained a reputation for excellent teaching in all subjects, but especially math. Close to 100 percent of the second- and third-grade youngsters regularly test proficient and advanced on state exams, followed by high performance of the upper grade students. Word has quickly spread that one really should go see their math instruction.

Weaver is one of six elementary schools in Los Alamitos. The district's forward-thinking leadership, including Superintendent Sherry Kropp, has brought about continuous growth and development of both teaching and learning throughout the system. Though many teachers at all six schools were already doing exemplary work, they felt there was always room for improvement and joined the Art of Teaching fellowship. Teachers like these illustrate how exceptional teaching can be continuously nurtured and grown in an environment which supports and even expects the highest levels of professional performance. The district has been using more of its best teachers in recent years to assist others as coaches.

A Major Redesign of Professional Development

At Alvarado Elementary School, we discovered additional talent to showcase great teaching. In contrast to Weaver Elementary, Alvarado sits in a lower-income neighborhood in the Signal Hill section of Long Beach, California. Many of the children come from Spanish-speaking homes, but the student body also includes groups of immigrants from Cambodia, Vietnam, and Laos. Many of the pupils are enrolled in special education classes, but spend part of their day in a regular classroom setting.

Alvarado's Sean Lindsay had been recommended as a teacher we should observe and perhaps utilize for demonstration lessons. Mr. Lindsay's teaching of Reader's Workshop and Writer's Workshop to upper-grade elementary children was indeed masterful. We could hardly wait for visiting teachers to see him in action. We heard that the forward-thinking principal had allocated money from the school budget for some faculty members, including Mr. Lindsay, to attend summer training in the workshop methods at Columbia

University's Teachers' College. The principal had also arranged for a coach from the college to spend a week assisting faculty at his elementary school.

Mr. Lindsay and his principal invited us to observe lessons taught by colleagues who had benefited from several years of training in the workshop methods. Their instruction was a joy to behold. These teachers also wanted more for themselves and their school and asked to join the Cotsen fellowship. During the next four years, two separate groups of the faculty participated as fellows, while some continued to host demonstration lessons. Mr. Lindsay applied and was chosen to be their mentor.

A couple of years after the fellowship ended at Alvarado, Dr. Brett Geithman, mentioned in the previous chapter, became principal and continued building upon the expertise of his faculty. He asked his teachers to help him redesign the school's professional development plan. Each faculty member chose to perfect one of three practices valued at the school—Reader's Workshop, Writer's Workshop, or CGI for mathematics in the primary grades. They organized themselves by grade level and content area. Teams met during time built into their weekly schedule. A few previous fellows who had developed expertise in a specific content area were asked to serve as coaches. Teams read books about these approaches and watched videos of teachers demonstrating the practices. They closely examined the techniques used and the skills being taught.

Coaches, released periodically from their own instruction, modeled lessons in team members' classes and observed their colleagues teaching. After observations, coaches encouraged each person to reflect on what worked well and determine what to tackle next. Teams developed assessments of student knowledge which they could implement and analyze on a daily or weekly basis. By noting what individual students were learning and which skills needed more work, they restructured lessons, adding more time for one-on-one conferences or for meeting with small clusters of kids in strategy groups to focus intensely on one skill. In math classes, students showed their peers different ways to go about solving the same problem, thereby illustrating a greater variety of solutions, and promoting more self-discovery of patterns and mathematical principles. The faculty formulated common goals while learning with and from each other. Designed with progressive student learning as the end goal, professional development had become a joint venture of the faculty and the principal.

With the hard work of the faculty and the excellent leadership of its principals, Alvarado students and their school performed remarkably well over the years, winning honors as a California Distinguished School and receiving Title I Academic Achievement Awards presented to high-achieving schools with large populations of children from low-income households. Alvarado continues to serve as a demonstration school visited by teachers from all parts of California.

A District-Wide Commitment

When Dr. Gregory Franklin joined Tustin Unified as superintendent, he immediately noticed that almost all the teachers in his system were hard-working individuals with great attitudes. He also realized there were no specific expectations and support for them to use practices that could very well benefit all students. Some elementary school teachers participating in the Art of Teaching were using the Writer's Workshop approach while others were working on comprehension skills using Reader's Workshop. A few fellows had introduced CGI for math to the primary grades.

Based on information gathered from the principals, the superintendent compiled a list of effective teaching practices already in use. Asked to recommend other practices, the secondary school principals suggested training in "Thinking Maps" to give students concrete images of abstract concepts such as "cause and effect." They also wanted to identify an effective method for teaching nonfiction writing. Faculty at each school were then asked to decide collectively which one "signature practice" from the list of recommended methods they would study and implement over a three-year span.

Dr. Franklin also sent a message to teachers and administrators urging them to clarify their mission and to strive for excellence—guiding principles he admired in the Art of Teaching professional development:

> We need to be really clear about what we do and why we do it. Let's all get expert at it. Let's make a commitment that we're not going to change course for three years at least. It's deeply rooted in the culture of the school that we're using whatever the signature practice is. It is just an expectation that we all speak the same language. The kids get it. The parents get it. We celebrate it. Once we can all look around and say, "We've got this one," then we are ready to add something more, whatever the something is.

These examples of professional development implemented at the school and district levels are not standard practices. They differ in their purposes, methods, quantity, and quality from prevalent professional development structures. As we have seen, practices like these lead to steady and dramatic improvements in instruction while boosting student participation and performance. None of this growth and development of teaching and learning could have happened without the complete commitment of principals and their superintendents. Great leadership nurtures and protects great teaching.

Box 7.1   Pause & Reflect

Resources are needed to promote continuous improvement including time, coaches, professional books, demonstration classes, and substitute time for Lesson Study and other collaborative work. What resources do your school and district provide to support a comprehensive professional learning program? What else is needed and how could those resources be allocated?

Continuous Learning by Principals

To be supporters and protectors of great teaching, principals and other district administrators benefit from understanding the research and the practices teachers select to advance student learning. Schools districts have hosted principals' meetings and invited providers of professional development to present introductions to practices like Reader's Workshop, Cognitively Guided Instruction, Shared Inquiry, and others. As a follow-up, curious principals chose to attend summer workshops on specific practices so that they could more thoroughly comprehend how teaching should proceed and what students might achieve. More often, principals went with their teachers to workshops and seminars on new practices their faculties found promising. The more knowledgeable and experienced principals are in the practice teachers are studying, the more they can comprehend why teachers are using the methods they do. They are in a better position to understand how complicated it is to implement the approaches with authenticity, and they are therefore much more likely to augment training enthusiastically with in-class coaching.

Sustaining the Impacts

When teachers within a school or a district have significantly improved instruction and attained higher levels of student achievement, they need to continue developing their strengths. There is no stopping point for learning how to improve. Maintaining a comprehensive professional development program is essential to avoid stagnation locally and to strengthen the field of education overall. Many training with coaching programs begin in schools and districts because of a grant or special program offering. These typically continue for a few years, and then when the funding disappears, so do the opportunities for teacher learning.

Kristin Gibson, currently a member of the board of education for Del Mar Union School District, declares that her district's professional development is sustained, systematic, and tied to what teachers are doing in the classroom so that they can understand how the practices benefit their students. "It does take resources," she adds. "It is hard for a group of teachers or a single principal to provide this kind of professional development by themselves. They need support from the system."

Under the best circumstances, districts embrace the growth teachers have achieved and continue the kind of professional development components which worked so well. Many districts will devote their own funding to professional training they had not supported before and offer coaching to teachers who choose to use that resource. Some have also created Professional Learning Communities to foster collaboration, made teaching more public through demonstration lessons, and encouraged teachers to join study groups or do action research.

Implementing a comprehensive professional development model with fidelity is essential if the enthusiasm, energy, and positive contagion teachers exhibited initially is to continue over decades. Fidelity means that school systems need to be careful not to spread the resources too thinly. Mentoring is effective if the coach works with a small group of teachers, and it loses most of its power when mentees are assigned large numbers of instructors. Saving money or sharing the resources equally across all teachers can result in losing ground. Typically, schools and districts need to choose whether teachers will select their content focus and set their own professional goals so that they are committed to them. At the other extreme, districts may press for all teachers to be teaching the same content each day in the same way so that all students at a grade level get exactly the same instruction. The latter choice tends to be both demoralizing and ineffective. Districts seeking coherence across classrooms should seek a balance between their goal and teacher participation in formulating a professional plan for growth. Coherence might best be achieved by empowering teachers to work in collaborative communities to research, test, and select the most effective teaching approaches to use with their students. Teacher "thought" and voice are perhaps the most vital elements of a successful professional development program which benefits students.

Summary

School and district leadership is key if teachers' engagement in their own learning is to result in enhanced student achievement on a large scale and be sustained over time. Principals, superintendents, and their staffs need to view teachers as professionals in charge of their own development. They need to see their best instructors as potential leaders who can help their colleagues grow. They must support collaborative learning, self-reflection, and continuous improvement with time, resources, and avid encouragement. They should also keep up to date on instruction and student learning themselves with additional training and observations. Most importantly, they must eschew short-term fixes, and instead do all in their power to sustain successful professional development practices year after year. By doing so, they will greatly enhance the performance of their teaching faculties and the accomplishments of their students.

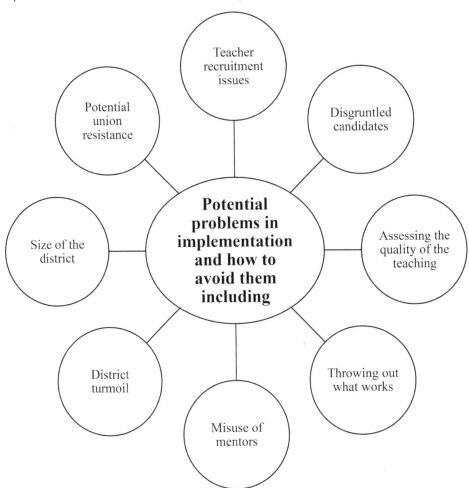

8

Obstacles along the Way

In undertaking a new and multifaceted endeavor, some setbacks are to be expected. I would like to describe a few problems we encountered setting up the Art of Teaching fellowship so that others who choose to implement a similar program, or components of it, can anticipate, and perhaps avoid, some of the difficulties.

Problems with Recruitment

In a few cases, we were frustrated with the results of our early recruitment efforts. Motivations to apply for a fellowship to study and enhance teaching varied, but selecting volunteers who were ready to take risks and try different methods seemed sensible. Their successes might show others that overcoming normal doubts and uncertainties could lead to remarkable achievements. Sometimes, however, we found it difficult to get the best teachers to step forward. Since most current mentoring programs have been designed for new teachers or those who need help, the experienced teachers were not sure that being coached was appropriate for them. Some others we hoped would apply were already heavily committed to extra duties at their schools or districts and not ready to take on more. A few teachers we thought might make excellent mentors were humble, self-critical, and doubted their qualifications for the job. Meanwhile, less skillful applicants did apply for the fellowship, perhaps to gain some recognition or achieve a higher status at their school.

After being chosen, and faced with the significant amount of time and dedication required, a small number balked at leaving the classroom, and failed to attend school visits and training sessions that could have enticed them to try something new in their classrooms.

The second time around, we altered our approach. Before presenting this professional learning program to the entire faculty, we asked principals to discuss the coming opportunity with their staff and explain how they perceived the training would work. We then gave our initial presentation to the school. Later in the week, teachers and mentors already participating in the program sat in the faculty lunchroom answering teachers' questions. They were also given contact information for other teachers in their districts who had offered to talk about the fellowship experience. Recruitment improved as teachers acquired information about the details of the program. Over time, the reputation of the Art of Teaching spread by word of mouth, and more of the school's most accomplished teachers applied for the fellowship at the next opportunity.

Disgruntled Candidates

On rare occasions, teachers who were not chosen for the fellowship showed signs of resentment toward those who were. Proactive principals acted before a problem arose and responded quickly when made aware of negative comments. To spread the beneficial effects of the program, administrators frequently provided funds to include a few non-participating teachers in classroom observations and training sessions. Principals also worked with the mentors to devise different ways for the fellows to share what they were learning with other faculty members. The influence of a few disgruntled individuals faded quickly as other faculty members became excited about what they saw those in the program doing and noticed the dramatic results teachers were getting with their students.

Assessing Quality Teaching Can Be Difficult

If students are involved in a lesson and the classroom is well managed, it can be difficult to assess the quality of instruction or to know what would help the teacher improve. Years ago, while observing a kindergarten reading lesson for second-language learners with one of our mentors, I realized again just how looks can be deceiving.

Performing in a dramatic fashion and utilizing colorful props, the teacher enthralled her young students. At the end of the story, the children went to assigned groups where they worked individually on several tasks with the aid of parent volunteers. Watching so many parents assisting in the class was impressive. Seeing this large class of very young, restless children listening respectfully during the reading and moving joyfully to their assignments felt right. At least it did until after we left the room, when the mentor asked me privately what it was that the children were learning in that lesson. What was the teaching point and how did the teacher know which students learned it and which did not? To be honest, going over my notes on the lesson, I could not answer those questions. Perhaps the objective was to introduce these youngsters to books and make reading interesting to them. Some of the children may have noticed the new vocabulary words the teacher put on the word wall, but they did not use those words themselves during the lesson, and there was no easily collectible evidence that they had learned something new. The assignments they were given immediately after the lesson did not appear to readily connect to a skill, or significantly reinforce information introduced during the reading. No methods for sounding out words or deciphering meaning had been demonstrated. Without asking for clarification from the teacher, I was uncertain about this lesson's purpose and its results. The parents and I had walked away from a class of happy children satisfied with a lesson that may have achieved the teacher's purpose or may not have taught even one child something they would remember and use in the future.

The best way to become adept at knowing what one is seeing in the classroom is to conduct a lot of observations. Chapter 1 includes a list of "Lenses for Observation" which has proved helpful. The more excellent teaching one sees, the more one will recognize what makes instruction effective and what impedes learning. With each visit, the observer should ask lots of questions. What is the teaching point of the lesson? How do the parts of the lesson contribute to students learning that teaching point? What are the responses of the individual students and what evidence shows that they have learned something new? Is the subject matter being taught appropriate for these students and does it match the content standards set by the district or the state? Finally, if uncertain about whether the instruction resulted in greater student understanding or skill, one should ask the teacher to clarify the specific goals of the lesson.

Throwing Out What Works

In their enthusiasm for new ideas and practices, a handful of teachers decided to throw out most, if not all, of the teaching methods or content they previously had used. This is not an uncommon response among educators, who frequently are expected to swing back and forth between teaching basic skills or abstract concepts, or between explicit instruction versus discovery methods of teaching, as the policy pendulum sways with district leadership. On occasion, a teacher will decide to throw the baby out with the bathwater, as it were, rather than to keep the best of different content and methods.

One mentor, who for the entire year had worked closely with a teacher on implementing strategies for improving reading comprehension, was surprised to find that many of the fellow's pupils had declined in their reading scores on the district's end-of-year tests. In discussing these disappointing results, the teacher revealed that she had stopped teaching basic skills in decoding and word recognition to allow more time for understanding the meaning of text. In her desire to teach more challenging material, she neglected the foundational skills her kids needed to master simultaneously. Teaching more difficult content is time consuming and requires that teachers realign their schedule to make room for the new instruction. Accomplished teaching requires a deep and thoughtful analysis of the wide range of knowledge and skills that students must acquire and build upon to keep growing academically.

Teachers learning how to use inquiry or project-based learning methods may be tempted to drop from their repertoire "direct instruction," a method proven to be efficient and effective. Generally, direct instruction refers to structured and sequenced teaching led by the teacher, using lectures, demonstrations, or modeling. This technique, when properly presented, involves establishing learning objectives for lessons, sequencing teaching to move students toward achieving those specific goals, giving clear explanations and illustrations of the knowledge and skills being taught, and checking in with students to determine the extent to which they understand the material. All these teaching approaches can be useful. Taking on new teaching methods must be done with a holistic view of the skills children need, and the preservation of basic and successful instructional strategies.

Misuse of Mentors

A fairly common problem is the misuse of a mentor's time by school officials. Mentors have sometimes been asked to fill in when substitute teachers fail to show up. Emergencies can be tolerated, but habitually interfering with the coaching schedule reduces the reliability and productivity of the mentor. Desperate for a helping hand, some principals have called on the mentor to perform other tasks, such as managing testing schedules and proctoring exams. In a few cases, weeks have been taken away from time designed to be spent coaching and attending professional development with the mentees.

Principals have also used a mentor as a confidante or even as a stand-in when the principal is temporarily unavailable. Changing the role in these ways can alter teachers' perception of the mentor, who to them may appear less devoted, less accessible, and less trustworthy. Nothing works smoothly when mentors cannot consistently perform their duties in ways their mentees have been told they can expect.

As tempting as it may be to have another knowledgeable person to assist with the assortment of tasks demanding immediate attention at a school, preserving the mentor's role and not cutting into the time needed to spend with his or her mentees will greatly improve the chances of the teachers achieving their long-range goals. The Art of Teaching principals have been very helpful by stressing to administrators new to the program the importance and benefits of respecting the mentor's agreed-upon duties.

District Turmoil

Turmoil in school districts creates a myriad of difficulties. It is especially antithetical to the development of quality teaching. When budgets are cut, teachers can be let go without consideration for the quality of their instruction, or they and their principals may be moved from site to site. During the most recent economic downturn, a district in California reassigned all 25 elementary school principals, and other massive changes followed. In another large school system, half the teachers at selected schools were moved to other schools because of turnover caused by layoffs and the seniority rules that govern assignments. Unsettling developments such as these made it almost impossible for teachers to concentrate on their own improvement, and left them with no consistent support from the school or the district. The nascent communities of teacher scholars dissolved. If teachers are to achieve greatness, they need to do so in a learning community with colleagues. They need to hear a consistent message from their school and district leaders that excellent teaching and improvements in student learning are priorities.

Fortunately, most principals and school district leaders participating in the Art of Teaching avoided or found ways to reduce the amount of turnover and "churn" in their schools. A few fortunate districts had hefty reserves to carry them through the years of budget drought. More enlightened district leaders steadfastly maintained quality instruction as their foremost concern, and worked diligently to keep the most successful principals and teachers in positions where they could continue to pursue greater academic achievements by their students.

Change in district or school leadership can also sabotage the momentum established by a comprehensive professional development program. As a new principal enters a school, he or she must be made fully aware that teachers themselves are leading the adult learning at the site and understand how that affects student performance. Often, the new school leader comes into a location ready to put in place curriculum and/or teaching methods with which he or she is most familiar. In more than one school, teachers have been told to stop what they were doing and change their approach as the new leadership arrived.

Similar changes in district administration have, at times, slowed the growth in teacher learning. For example, several years ago a new associate superintendent for curriculum and instruction took over in one small district in California. She ordered all principals to stop using whatever teaching methods they currently had in place and to replace them with one approach she preferred. District staff visited classrooms to make sure that teaching across all schools conformed to the associate superintendent's mandate. More than 50 elementary school teachers eventually marched to a school board meeting to ask for an opportunity to describe how methods they had learned to use proficiently in the previous few years had produced excellent results for children. They made it clear that they were reluctant to change to another approach with no explanation, rationale, or consultation. The energies of teachers, unfortunately, had to shift for a period of time toward resisting their leaders rather than maintaining the continuous development of their teaching craft in which they had been engaged.

The Size of School Districts

In large districts, the enthusiasm and impact of our first efforts with a few schools did not spread widely. We had a strategy of reaching a critical mass of teachers by offering the fellowship in 80 percent or more of the schools. This worked well in small and moderately-sized districts. In Los Angeles Unified, with its hundreds of elementary schools and thousands of teachers, the program had difficulty establishing a firm foothold. Nevertheless, groups of teachers within individual schools in L. A. Unified and other large school systems have benefited from the fellowship, and the entire teaching faculty has improved when a principal leveraged the work of the fellows to inspire and train other teachers. However, without a strong system-wide commitment to the professional development program from the start, it remains difficult in larger districts to create momentum across a substantial number of schools. Creating a small cluster of participating schools located close to each other within the larger district, and building networks of the administrators and teachers across these schools, can help to establish a learning community of adults who strengthen and sustain the development of quality teaching.

Possible Union Resistance

An early concern about resistance from teachers' unions was a potential obstacle which, in our case, failed to materialize. We structured the Art of Teaching to support teachers while avoiding many of the issues which worry their union leadership, such as tying the fellowship to teacher evaluations, directing teachers in how they must teach, or creating a different pay scale for mentors. Before the program started in a school system, we asked that the superintendent have district staff meet with union leaders to inform them about the program, answer their questions, and obtain their blessing. Teachers and union leaders from other districts volunteered to explain how the fellowship had worked for them and answer questions. These same individuals were especially helpful reassuring their union compatriots and leaders that the fellowship was providing many substantial benefits to its teachers and to their schools as well.

Box 8.1   Pause & Reflect

If you were to improve upon your school's or district's professional development plan, what obstacles might you encounter and how would you attempt to prevent them from occurring?

Summary

Things can get in the way of fully implementing a comprehensive professional development program like the one we recommend in this book. It may help to try different approaches, as we did with our recruitment efforts and our tools to assess what we observe in classrooms.

Harder to anticipate and overcome has been the various types of turmoil. When faced with unanticipated economic challenges, district officials must try, at all costs, to retain teachers and principals who have dedicated themselves to more effective instruction for all their pupils.

Standardized test scores

Examples of how comprehensive professional development has worked and the elements which have improved including

Effects on schools

Student productivity and independence

Changes in teaching and in teachers

9

Measuring Success

Comprehensive professional development affects the quality of teaching and student learning in numerous ways. The measures used to assess those effects should be diverse enough to capture the wide array of results. In this chapter, I include evaluation data from 15 years of the Art of Teaching fellowship to illustrate changes and improvements one might expect from a professional development program with similar features. Hundreds of observations in classrooms and on video recordings, plus in-depth interviews and surveys of teachers, administrators, and students, provide much of the evidence. First, I need to touch on the issue of test scores.

Standardized Tests

Standardized test scores are one way of measuring the effects of teaching on student learning, though improving these test scores was not a primary aim of the Art of Teaching. At the start, we were looking for changes in teaching and student classroom performance. We felt that comparing pretest and post-test scores of students whose teachers were in the fellowship with those who were not in the program was unlikely to be statistically significant because our sample sizes were small, and the teachers were spread across grade levels and a range of subject matter. Even so, one evaluation conducted by an external consulting group did show a link between professional development and student learning in the form of a greater growth in test scores for students of teachers in the program as compared with others.

During the 2013–2014 school year, the first year Culver City Unified School District implemented the mentoring program, students in kindergarten and first grade took a district math assessment, the only standardized test available, as a pretest and post-test. The primary grade children in the six Art of Teaching classes (109 students at two schools) had significantly higher mean post-test scores than students in comparison classes with teachers who were non-participants (Kohne, Mechlinski, and Schmalstig 2014, 42). This was true even though their mean pretest scores were lower than those of comparison students. All children in the Art of Teaching classes came from Title I schools and many of them lived in low-income households. This was not the case with comparison classes.

The conclusion of the evaluators was that students with teachers involved in a comprehensive program to learn about mathematics instruction outperformed those in comparison classes, and that this was particularly true for the first-grade pupils. The significant growth in math scores for students continued into the 2014–2015 school year. The results from test data, student interviews and observations, teaching observations and teacher surveys, confirm that this comprehensive professional development program contributed to the higher performance of the children.

Student Productivity and Independence

The evidence for growth in student achievement can be seen in classrooms long before end-of-year standardized tests can validate its occurrence. Student performance and classroom behaviors tell us children are already engaged in activities which are nourishing their academic and personal growth. Teachers and principals have described what's different in the children's behavior. They see students more involved in lessons and more productive. Pupils demonstrate greater independence and self-responsibility for being a learner.

The mentor at Northam Elementary in Rowland Heights, George Herrera, asked his mentees for their impressions after viewing videos of their lessons taken at the beginning and toward the end of their fellowships. Kindergarten teacher Liz Rios spoke of the differences in behavior and attitudes she detected in students during her two years. Using Reader's Workshop and Writer's Workshop methods, she had spent the first couple of months of the previous school year carefully laying the groundwork for new ways students could approach their assignments and work more collaboratively. In the second year-end video, she saw the progress her next group of five- and six-year-old pupils had made. Ms. Rios talked about how her students had become far more engaged in reading after they were encouraged to choose the books they wanted to read from an appropriate selection she offered them.

> These kids can be independent and have taken so much responsibility. They are so involved in books. They are so much more capable than I ever thought they were. They were taking ownership of their own learning. They were so intense! Their talk was all about what they were doing. That's a change. In the first video, there was more of me and less of them. In the second video, I saw more of them and less of me.

Working with mentors to implement a curriculum designed to have students dive deeply into content and develop critical thinking skills, teachers frequently discover that they are doing too much of the classroom work and their pupils want to do more of it on their own. Their students want more challenges, choices, and opportunities to share their discoveries with others than they are usually given. Children flourish under conditions where they feel more in control. They grow in their confidence and begin to view themselves as self-directed, self-managed learners.

When interviewed, students told us about the teaching going on in classrooms and how they react to it. Children in the upper elementary grades at McGaugh Elementary in Los Alamitos described how their teachers had set higher expectations, asking them to tackle difficult tasks and to work responsibly with others.

"She asks us challenging questions," one child explained.

Another said, "She tells us to turn around and talk to each other so we can share our own thinking." When asked why that would be important, the child replied, "So if somebody didn't think of it and they thought a different idea, they could know what you are thinking and I could know what they are thinking."

"What important things do you notice about your work as mathematicians?" another teacher asked her class.

Three of their comments give evidence of greater independence in the children and reveal some critical attitudes about the teaching they had experienced in prior years:

One student responded, "You can think of your own efficient strategies. More and more ideas pop in my head every second. We can think for ourselves."

Otis complained about his previous classroom experiences. "Teachers are like, 'I'm the boss of you.' They tell us, 'You do this. You do that.' The kids have a great idea, but they don't let them do it. The teachers are like, 'No. You cannot do that. You have to do this.'"

Tanya added, "We do thinking for ourselves because we are smart enough. We have our own brains. We can control our bodies. We don't just have to be lazy. We don't have to have the teacher do it and us be lazy. It's like the teacher is doing our homework. Like the teacher is doing our math. Like the teacher is doing our reading. The teacher is doing everything for us."

Changes in Teaching and in Teachers

The essential question behind the mission of the Art of Teaching was whether good teachers could learn to become great. To ascertain how much change had occurred, the staff examined each person's four teaching videos. Using our professional judgment and paying attention to elements in our "Lenses for Observation," we concluded that there were visible and important improvements for at least 80 percent of the participating teachers. In fact, we identified about one-fifth of the graduates as teaching so artfully that they could easily qualify for the role of demonstration teachers.

The quality of the mentoring appears to be associated with the degree of change in a teacher's practice. The most successful mentors helped every individual significantly move up the scale toward high-quality teaching. Effective mentors mobilized the teachers to participate in every activity offered to them. The teachers enjoyed each other's company and worked well together as a team in inquiry or in small groups pursuing common interests. Fellows spoke highly of these mentors and emphasized how helpful they had been. Less effective mentors found it difficult to get the fellows to go on observations, attend follow-up training, or participate constructively in inquiry meetings. In those few cases, most of their fellows performed very much the same on videos for both years. More frequently, however, we found that only one of the five to eight fellows on certain school teams failed to move forward, and that seemed to be for a variety of other reasons, such as an illness in the family or other personal problems.

Both teaching and teachers change because of the fellowships. We have seen how they invest more time and care in thoroughly planning instruction. They discover new ways to fully engage the children as they teach. They get students to talk more about the ways they understand the material. More effective small-group and one-on-one instruction, better questioning techniques, more purposeful conversations among students, building on children's strengths, encouraging them to persist until they succeed, incorporating analysis and evaluative thinking into assignments—these are all signs that excellent teaching has emerged. As teachers become more successful with students, they also become more confident and willing to try new approaches.

When asked how much growth they have made, teachers leave no doubt that something significantly different has occurred in their classrooms. The following stories illustrate those changes.

I am still learning and changing.

After observing how Cognitively Guided Instruction encourages students to become more creatively involved in solving problems, a veteran teacher with a strong interest in mathematics decided to totally revamp his approach to teaching that subject. After his 37th year in teaching, he told us:

> I learned that there was a whole system of strategic planning, lots of reflection, and very purposeful thought that had to go into my math instruction. It has taken some trial and error but that's how I made it work for me. What I have learned has been a shift of how I teach math and how I look at my students. It doesn't happen overnight and I'm still learning and changing.

No more tears!

Another teacher wrote a lengthy response to a survey asking about how she and her students changed:

> I am a completely different teacher when it comes to writing. Not only have my lessons changed, but my teaching philosophy has done a 360. I allow time for the writing process and put so much more value on all the things my students are doing right. It is a very respectful approach to teaching writing and my kids are more excited to write than ever before. I used to have a few students every year who would simply, and literally, cry when it was writing time. They would shut down, say "I don't know how," and were too embarrassed or too insecure to even try. Now I have confident writers who are each writing at very different levels but who are consistently, but gently, guided to strive for their personal best. No more tears!

One cannot easily describe changes in teachers without mentioning the effect on their students, some of which we have already seen. The following comments show in greater detail how teachers have changed their instruction and how they, too, have personally changed. They also illustrate ways that their students' attitudes and abilities have developed.

Student success is my battery charger.

Renee Shelly Keasey, a special education teacher at Mar Vista Elementary in Pajaro Valley Unified School District, taught for 11 years before her fellowship began. She explained how much she had changed over those two years and how proud she was of her students:

> I honestly feel as if I've been given a teacher makeover—at least in the realm of writing, which is my focus area. I sometimes think back to the early years of my career. I was fresh out of my credential program, my teacher toolbox was full, and I couldn't wait to use all those tools with enthusiasm. Then, as time passed, I tended to fall into a pattern of teaching and I didn't challenge myself very often to try new methods. I'm so grateful for the training I've received and for the relationships I've formed. Not only has my practice been transformed, but my mind and the way I think about best practices in education has been renewed. I feel as if student success is my battery charger and those moments of being fully charged feel awesome, especially during this time of year when most of us feel drained on a daily basis!
>
> When our team members were selected, we all felt so honored. The idea of being so incredibly supported by our mentors, administrators, and our colleagues felt special. But, I admit I still had reservations. Change can put fear in us, can't it? I wasn't sure what it really meant to 'teach artfully' and I hoped that my practice would measure up. . . . One huge fear of mine had to do with the ability levels of my special education students. When we first started observing other teachers who were implementing Writer's Workshop, we were blown away and excited to try their strategies. Then, fear would creep in again and I'd tell myself things like, "I'll have to modify every part of those lessons" or "My students probably won't fully get that concept." Well, shame on me, teacher of little faith.
>
> Let's fast-forward to what I reflect on now. I mostly think about all of the heart-warming experiences I've had with my students. I think about Loni coming back from the library one day saying,

"Mrs. Keasy, here's a book written by the same author that we studied yesterday. Can we read this too?" I also think about Mark, who in the beginning of the year showed me his first Writer's Workshop seed story. It was a string of about 12 to 15 letters. Now, I've become pretty skilled in deciphering some pretty tricky writing samples, but I honestly had no idea what he intended to write in that entry—nor did he. Throughout this year, he has cried on more than one occasion stating, "Don't you get it? I can't read! I can't do this!" He kept trying though. A couple of weeks ago, when we began our memoir writing unit, that kid sat down on day one of the unit and wrote the most beautiful, tear-jerking story about the day when he was told that his beloved dog, Fox, had passed away. His piece was descriptive. It included dialogue and internal thoughts and feelings. I could go on. I had no trouble reading that entry. I think about the way my students have, on occasion, taken their writer's notebooks to recess so that they could show the principal their work. It's safe to say that none of my students liked writing before their introduction to Writer's Workshop. They hated it because they had never experienced success in writing. Now, I see these confident children who call themselves writers. They are so very proud and so am I. What more could I have wanted?

I think my colleagues would agree that now we all do understand what it means to teach artfully. We don't want this journey to end. We plan to keep meeting and collaborating so that we can all continue to grow, sharpen our skills, and learn new ones.

Instead of "good little listeners," I now have a class of critics.

An upper-grade special education teacher, Becky Mandell at McGaugh Elementary in Los Alamitos Unified School District, spoke about how she changed in her teaching and how her students changed as learners:

When I think about my teaching two years ago, I have to smile and shake my head. I was a good teacher. My favorite time was story time. I loved to get my students sitting on the rug, legs folded, hands in their laps, smiles on their faces, and eyes on me. I would even say that to them. I could entertain and hold the attention of the toughest behavior cases. I was in complete control. My mentor challenged me to let go of some of the control. I started introducing metacognition. While reading to them, I would ask them to wonder out loud. After just one book, they were starting to wonder amazing things. Story time had been transformed into literature analysis time. The kids now come to the rug with a clipboard, a stack of Post-Its and a pencil. I can't even get through the first page of a book and they're already writing on their Post-Its like crazy. Instead of "good little listeners," I now have a class of critics.

Ms. Mandell built on her passion for reading and found ways to make her special education students active participants in story time. She helps them articulate what they notice, how the author told the story, and what they found of interest in the characters as they changed over time. Her students not only listen to the books Ms. Mandell reads to them, but they also have developed a new relationship with the content. They are actively analyzing and evaluating the stories.

The fellowship pushed me to do things I never would have done.

With knowledge and growth, teachers become more confident. They have taken on roles as leaders in their schools. Kristy Parra reflected on how she had changed personally and how her teaching fellowship influenced all parts of her life. After working with her mentor at Garfield Elementary School in Long Beach, she accepted a position as a facilitator helping teachers at nearby Webster Elementary, something she thought she would never do. At California State University at Long Beach, she applied and was accepted into the Master's and credential program for school administrators. When she qualified for her school district's Aspiring Vice Principal program, she readily took that next step. She says that through the fellowship she improved her teaching, her reflectiveness, and her willingness to try new things: "It pushed me to do things I never would have done, and in the process made me a better person and a better educator."

Box 9.1   Pause & Reflect

How do you currently measure the effectiveness of your school's or district's professional learning program? What other potential outcomes would you like to measure to make sure your program does what you want it to do for teachers, students, the school, and the district?

Effects on Schools

With the help of committed principals, groups of inspired teachers have helped to change their entire school into a more collaborative community focused on continuous improvement. In Chapter 5, Principal Geithman of Alvarado Elementary praised the change of culture in his school that resulted from the Cotsen experience. Here, three additional principals discuss how they established a different school environment with the aid of faculty who had completed the Art of Teaching fellowship.

Mitchell became a place where people wanted to be.

When Lucia Laguarda came to Billy Mitchell Elementary School as principal in 2002, she pretty much started from scratch to build up the school's performance. Situated in a predominantly Spanish-speaking neighborhood near Los Angeles International Airport, Mitchell had the dubious distinction of being the lowest scoring elementary campus in the district on state tests. The year before she arrived, a half-time mentor began coaching four teachers in the Art of Teaching fellowship. In following years, other colleagues joined, and by 2010 a total of 15 faculty members had participated. Some eventually left to take care of young children, moved to a different school in Lawndale, or took another job. The remaining eight teachers, about a third of the faculty, continued to have a great influence. With these teachers and a principal who wanted to build upon their strengths, Mitchell became a different school. It rose from the poorest performer in Lawndale to become the school with the greatest gains on state tests. Teachers opened their classrooms and Billy Mitchell became a demonstration site for teachers in their district and from other school systems as well.

Principal Laguarda described how she worked with her teachers and how their performance changed the school's achievement:

> The teachers and their test score data showed who they were. If the same kids had a year of a poor teacher, they ended up flat. I balanced those kids so they would have a good teacher after they had a flat year. Those who had Cotsen teachers in grades K, 1, 2—those kids did well in grades 3 to 5, even if they didn't have a good teacher in those later years. They had been taught to be readers, writers, thinkers. There was growth at Mitchell from the lowest performing school in the district to the school with the most growth in reading, writing, math, and for English language learners. Mitchell became a place

where people wanted to be. It had been the stepchild of the district. Now, families and staff wanted their own kids there.

The ideal way for teachers to learn and grow.

Miriam Kim became principal of the aptly-named Telesis, a new K-8 school in Rowland Heights, after serving as principal at an elementary school participating in the Art of Teaching. Telesis means a deliberate, purposeful utilization of the processes of nature and society to obtain particular goals, and Kim's goal was for every child to succeed. The most valuable part of the Art of Teaching, she notes, was "the trickle up, down, and all-around effect." All teachers, including her fellows, were asked to join her at Telesis to help shape the way the school approached instruction.

> I have teachers who have not had any training or exposure to Reader's or Writer's Workshop. But because they see the work that their colleagues around them are doing, they ask questions and are implementing this work in their own classes. The elementary teachers were so strongly equipped that when they moved up to the middle school grades they brought all of those wonderful strategies to the older students. The fellowship helped to break down the walls to learning and encouraged everyone to see each other as seekers of knowledge on an even playing field. We all agree that this is the ideal way for teachers to learn and grow. In light of many schools beginning to go K-8, and the studies that are coming out regarding middle schools and how they are the last bastion of hope for change, I would like to see more support and thought given to our middle school grades. I believe that this approach to supporting teachers will have a tremendous effect for our junior high colleagues.

It's an absolute belief that if you invest in the skill, in the person, in the teacher, you will get results that stream down to the kids.

Maggie Villegas, principal at Arroyo Elementary in Tustin, saw important results for her entire school from four years in the Art of Teaching. By usual measures, the school had been performing well, with test scores above 900 on the Academic Performance Index (API) that topped out at 1,000. As those scores continued to rise, it was not those measurements that impressed her most. She saw that the teachers had become involved in a different kind of dialogue about their students. As she put it, "It's been all about the learning." Her teachers had learned about the relationship triangle connecting the teacher's passion for the subject, the students' engagement in study, and the rigorous content itself. They recognized that while they were studying how to improve their teaching and were going deeper into the content to be taught, the real target was student learning. "You can teach the most masterful lesson and you might have ten kids who still didn't learn your teaching point. Our teachers are now exceptionally capable of looking at these kids in this different way and adapting what they are doing to fit these children." In an interview, she elaborated:

> This has completely elevated these people who are so deserving as professionals to have that investment in them. They think, "I'm a professional who has mastered this content area. I've studied it. I've invested in it. I've talked about it." We've dialogued about it. We share in our staff meetings about content. What's important is that a teacher walks into that classroom ready to teach a math lesson with vigor and rigor and is excited. I've seen teachers have kids engaged in discussions that weren't taking place before. I watched 41 fourth-graders have a "Grand Conversation" in our multipurpose room about a chapter book that they read and the teacher was completely a bystander. The kids dialogued and led the conversation. That's intentional and artful instruction, which does not happen if a teacher is not gifted at bringing that out in those kids.
>
> We used the Art of Teaching as a whole-school model. We used it to unify our mission and our purpose so that our discussion about kids and my discussion with my teachers about kids is not just about their kids in their rooms. But, we have said that if these teachers went out and saw this incredible math instruction, why don't we want it for every single kid here, grades K through 5. My role as a principal has been to bring that visional piece and let everybody know that everybody is capable of doing this. Every teacher! We can support you and give you the steps to get there. We just must all be on board. We have done steps here to let teachers go in and watch each other, even on our own campus, so that they were able to watch the kids from K, 1, 2, 3. They walked out of a third-grade class and said, "No child can fail." If our continuity between our classes in K through grade 3 is this consistent and concise, with our use of language and our dialogue and our practices that we are doing, there is not a bad classroom to be in. Every one of these classes—there would be no way a child could not get through and fail to become an exemplary student because of the teaching.

From a district perspective, we haven't been pushing ourselves to make sure our teachers are out seeing others teach. I have been a principal for 11 years and this is the first year I've had colleagues visit. The process, structure, and support system is showing us all the best approach to keep our teachers moving.

It's not a program. It's not a focus on something you can tangibly get and bring back to your site. It's an absolute belief that if you invest in the skill, in the person, in the teacher, you will get results that stream down to the kids. You can't undervalue what that means when a teacher walks away, in her heart and mind feeling validated as a professional.

Ms. Villegas is not alone in her conclusion that those very good teachers who became fellows affected the teaching of others by word of mouth and by being public in their teaching. Principal after principal has affirmed in interviews and surveys that the involvement of a critical mass of teachers in the fellowship ended up influencing their entire school. As individual teachers moved along the path of continuous improvement, they were more successful with their students, and their successes generated in others an enthusiasm to learn more and achieve even better results.

Summary

A comprehensive approach to professional development has the power to revitalize teaching and teachers, change student behaviors and achievement, plus alter school cultures. Changes you could hope to see resulting from this kind of professional learning include:

- ◆ Improvements in the efficiency and efficacy of instruction.
- ◆ Presentation of more challenging content and more opportunities for students to analyze, critique, evaluate, and apply the subject material they learn.
- ◆ Increased student engagement in learning and interest in the subject matter.
- ◆ Greater student productivity and persistence when dealing with difficult tasks.
- ◆ Greater student knowledge of content and academic skills.
- ◆ Development of a collaborative school culture where teachers make teaching public and share what they learn with peers.

To assess the effects of a school's or district's professional learning program, it helps to examine what is different for all involved—students, faculty, administrators, and even parents. Instruments and data sources to consider using include:

- Participation of faculty in professional development options.
- Surveys and interviews of students, teachers, administrators, parents.
- Classroom observations of teaching.
- Classroom observations of student engagement and productivity.
- Samples of student work.
- Samples of lesson plans and classroom assessments of student learning.
- District and state test scores.

Reference

Lisa Kohne, Timothy Mechlinski, and Mariana Schmalstig. 2014. "Evaluation of the Mathematics Leadership Corps Program: Quarter 1 Evaluation Report." Unpublished Evaluation Report. Irvine, CA: SmartStart Evaluation and Research.

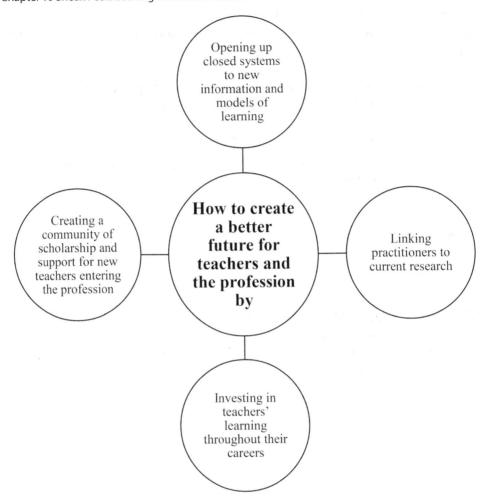

10

Looking toward the Future

Good teachers can and do learn to be great at their craft. We have seen how comprehensive programs of professional development have helped teachers from a wide range of elementary schools become exceptionally effective educators. Their students have become more enthusiastic, independent, and successful learners because of great teaching. Shouldn't every child be educated in this way by expert teachers?

Providing similar opportunities on a much wider scale will require a change in attitudes about teaching, as well as different expectations of teachers and administrators. School systems will need to institute a more productive program of professional development that enables teachers to improve the quality of their instruction at every stage of their careers.

Opening Closed Systems

Education in the United States typically functions as a closed and highly localized system. Teachers in far too many schools operate for extended time periods independent of one another, except for planning the broad outlines of what will be taught and occasionally sharing new curriculum they discover. Being in each other's classes when students are present remains a rare event. Even within districts, principals rarely have a chance to ask instructors from another school to share their successful strategies. Districts, instead, more often compete for pupils rather than cooperate on providing opportunities for mutually beneficial professional learning.

School districts develop customs—certain ways of doing business which vary from place to place and which can be both an asset and a liability. Unless district teachers attend workshops and seminars sponsored by well-respected external organizations, or keep up to date on research about both teaching and learning, their knowledge is circumscribed by what they see and hear from district trainers. In some school systems, a dearth of professional development opportunities has for years left educators to rely on their own resources to advance their learning. In others, the training provided is at least more consistent and sometimes proves useful. Seeking and embracing ideas and practices that can create greater enthusiasm and elevate the achievement levels of more students should be a major objective of all district administrators.

Even within small school systems, it should be possible to identify a handful of teachers who are very successful with children and whose practices in at least one content area deserve emulation. Why not open the classroom doors to all educators within every school? From observations of others' teaching, faculty members may discover a colleague who knows how to design instruction based on the level of readiness of individual pupils. Perhaps they will find other instructors who know more about science or social studies than they do, someone who could be used as a resource for constructing more challenging lessons. They may encounter a teacher who is particularly good at teaching art and integrating that subject into history, literature, or music. Each school can build its collective strength by forming collaborations among its own best teachers and those who want or need to learn from the strengths of others. Across schools within the same district one may find far more resources and inspirational teaching. Larger school systems have the advantage of a wider talent pool. A wellspring of knowledge might easily be acquired from educators located only blocks away or just across town. Presently, much of that talent is underutilized.

The resources for teacher learning are often right in front of us. It may be as simple as shifting highly effective teachers into a new role, such as a mentor or teacher trainer, so colleagues can benefit from their expertise. Using the resources within a system to build better teaching is only a beginning. To approach greatness, more is required. The reasonable next step would be to seek other innovative ideas outside the district, from the research community and high-performing schools. Broadening the scope to explore the work of great teachers and programs beyond district borders may lead to an abundance of new and different approaches that could greatly enhance both teaching and learning.

Utilizing Research Findings

Some of us imagine researchers as people far removed from our everyday reality. We may think they spend too much time dealing with subjects of minimal significance. In fact, educational research has given us a flood of information and new understanding. We know so much more now than in past decades about learning disabilities, how memory works, and how very young children process information. One useful example is the 15 years of research reported in *Children's Mathematics: Cognitively Guided Instruction*, authored by Thomas P. Carpenter *et al.* (2015). CGI is referenced many times in *Building Effective Professional Development in Elementary School* because so many teachers have found the approach so remarkable. Carpenter's book describes how children think about number concepts while solving problems, and how they connect their informal knowledge with formal concepts and operations taught in school. The book is also practical as it provides concrete examples of how to teach to build upon children's informal knowledge.

Linking practitioners to research findings on more effective teaching methods should not be difficult. However, in *From the Ivory Tower to the Schoolhouse: How Scholarship Becomes Common Knowledge in Education* (2014), Jack Schneider cites several barriers. A lack of support from school districts is one. Another is the absence of time in the teaching day for scholarship. A cultural bias which views teachers as content deliverers, rather than as thoughtful users of education resources, also weakens the link between the worlds of research and practice. Schneider places some of the blame on research studies that are not relevant, practical, and usable for the classroom. He admonishes researchers to use more accessible language so that structures like curriculum frameworks and specific training strategies discussed in the research can more readily be put in place. He also stresses a critical point that our work has confirmed:

> There is no escaping the centrality of teachers—at least with regard to what happens once the bell rings, students take their seats, and classroom doors swing shut. Accordingly, reformers seeking to improve the instructional core in education must cultivate educators as willing and able partners, working collectively to expand what teachers know.
> (Schneider 2014, 207)

Investing in Teachers

Teachers do not enter their profession as experts. First, they must master the basic elements of their field. Over time, some may become exceptional educators. The greatest number of teachers become continuously more effective over their first ten years of practice. And surprisingly, recent research shows that teachers improved in their ability to boost test scores by 40 percent between the tenth and the thirtieth year on the job (Papay and Kraft, 2016). Just imagine what teachers could achieve if they and their school systems made career-long commitments to the continuous improvement of teaching through a comprehensive and sustained program of professional learning. Just imagine the children in their classes fully engaged, achieving more, demonstrating advanced skills and deeper knowledge, persisting when faced with challenging tasks, and fully active and responsible for their own learning.

For decades, education experts, school reformers, parents, and politicians have been clamoring for schools to do a better job of educating America's youth and improving the quality of instruction. Two approaches have long been in vogue. One tries to eliminate the influence of individual teachers by "teacher proofing" instruction using technology or scripted curriculum. The other issues rewards or punishments to teachers based on results demonstrated by their students, usually on standardized tests. Conversations about reforming schools use words and phrases such as accountability, testing, teacher evaluations, vouchers, and even "blowing up the system." These notions focus on external levers for change, which miss the mark because they neither inspire teachers nor engage them as a force for change and educational improvement.

Most of us yearn for a sense of meaning, fulfillment, and accomplishment in our workplace. This is especially true of a multitude of teachers who are drawn to their profession because they want to contribute to bettering the future of young people and, by extension, our larger society. They, like the rest of us, want to make a difference with their lives and their work. This strong motivation can overcome the fears that may naturally arise when educators are asked to try something new and to strive to achieve success for every youngster in their care. Teachers are the heartbeat of successful schools. They, more than any other factor in the education equation, have the most direct influence on student achievement. If teachers are to reach for and achieve excellence in their profession, and thereby improve student learning, the school systems themselves must change.

Standing in the way of teachers striving for excellence is the absence of continuous and meaningful professional development programs, which essentially limits their exposure to new research and developing teaching practices. When teachers observe excellent instruction and then say, "I didn't know what I didn't know," they are telling us that they have had insufficient access to information about effective pedagogical techniques and the content they are teaching. They make it clear that had they known more, they could have been more effective in raising their students' levels of achievement. The lack of opportunities to interact with professionals, in their own schools and elsewhere, who are using methods and curriculum that can truly inspire children, will always hinder and even preclude their growth into artful educators.

We have shown that a comprehensive model of professional development, such as the Art of Teaching, or the Teacher Development Group's CGI training, and other programs using many of the same essential components, can strengthen teaching. This kind of professional development invests in the best teachers first and builds on their strengths. It offers training in deeper subject matter content and the pedagogy linked to that content. It provides coaching while teaching, as well as time for working with others on tasks such as lesson-planning and its refinement. It also arranges visits to the classes of exemplary teachers and dialogue with them about the effects of their methodologies on children's learning. It encourages them to aspire to achieve excellence as a teacher, and to become a lifelong scholar collaborating with other practitioners. All of this should take place in an environment free of formal evaluation and one that emphasizes the value of progressive improvement. Most importantly, the teachers themselves should be encouraged to set the goals and control the direction of their intellectual growth and advancement of their teaching abilities.

Clearly, there is more than one right way to teach, but the best approach to betterment for an individual teacher must encompass his or her personal style and passion for the subjects being taught. Styles of effective teaching vary—dramatic, Socratic, autocratic, democratic—to name a few. All can succeed if they build upon a strong foundation of knowledge and persuasive skills, a combination that is certain to expand the horizons and achievements of the students in front of them.

To revitalize teaching careers and produce these kinds of results for students that school district leaders would hope to achieve, many things must change. First, district administrators and education policymakers must help alter the image of teaching by treating educators as professionals. That means that continuous professional development should become an integral component of a teaching career. More school districts will need to develop teacher leaders, and establish a nurturing and collaborative environment in which educators increase their understanding of teaching with each other's help.

Second, system leaders must change both the content and the structure of professional development so that it is long term, continuous, and connected to unfamiliar or new research studies on approaches to teaching. Professional development must engage teachers as designers and active participants in their own learning, and help them set their own rigorous professional goals. Opportunities for them to work collaboratively with colleagues and other distinguished practitioners must be provided. Classrooms should be viewed as learning laboratories in which teachers can practice with a coach and observe their fellow instructors. Building a common base of knowledge about practices that work should become a primary aim of collaborative faculty learning.

Third, superintendents and board members need to supply the resources necessary to organize and support this type of learning. This would include setting aside ample time in the school calendar for professional development, arranging individual and group training conducted by district staff or noteworthy external organizations, and purchasing classroom and professional materials to support implementation of new or different methods. A key component will be for systems to identify and train mentors, coaches, and demonstration teachers, and offer them a schedule which permits them to work intensively with small numbers of teachers over extended periods of time.

Conclusion

The answer we found to the question raised at the beginning of this book is "Yes!" Good teachers can achieve greatness. Even those who do not reach artful levels of instruction can refine their craft and significantly improve student performance. I cannot envision a more opportune time to invest in these types of change, the implementation of which could make high-quality teaching more the norm.

Currently, public education is losing large numbers of its seasoned teachers, and novices are taking their places. Historically, a huge proportion of elementary and secondary educators have left the profession in the first few years of their career. The problem of turnover has become even more discouraging in recent years. In the late 1980s, most of the country's three million K-12 public school teachers had more than a decade of experience. By 2008, according to national government workforce statistics, the median number of years on the job had shrunk to just one year (Ingersoll, Merrill, and Stuckey 2014, 12). With so many neophytes coming on board, and given that it generally takes about five years to develop teaching competence, the revolving door of a teaching career has become a dire concern.

New instructors will require help just to become adequate at their jobs. More effort must be directed toward keeping the most promising new hires. A revitalized and more appealing teaching profession will attract them and certainly encourage them to stay. A new generation of educators deserves a profession that supports their learning and growth over an entire career. Transforming schools into small communities of scholars, and linking teachers with individuals and groups with whom they can share knowledge and insights, will greatly assist them, and quite possibly lengthen their years of service.

This type of professional learning is not a quick fix for school reform, but it addresses problems in the quality of teaching and learning by focusing attention directly on what happens in classrooms. Infusing our public educational system with higher quality teaching will require time and commitment from the individual teacher, the school team, and the system itself. The dramatic results in student motivation, behavior, and achievement that will follow are well worth the investment.

Developing schools in which every student is engaged, every student learns, and every student gains a sense of personal power should be the aim of every community. To enhance our public schools and fulfill this vision, we need to open more doors of opportunity to teachers, allow them to see exemplary instructors at work, instill in them a desire to achieve greater heights, and provide them the tools and resources they need to become ever more artful at their craft.

References

Carpenter, Thomas P., Elizabeth Fennema, Megan Loef Franke, Linda Levi, and Susan B. Empson. 2015. *Children's Mathematics: Cognitively Guided Instruction.* Portsmouth, NH: Heinemann.

Ingersoll, Richard M., Lisa Merrill, and Daniel Stuckey. 2014. "Seven Trends: The Transformation of the Teaching Force, Updated April 2014." *CPRE Report (#RR-80).* Philadelphia: Consortium for Policy Research in Education, University of Pennsylvania.

Papay, John P. and Mathew A. Kraft. 2016. "The Myth of the Performance Plateau." *Educational Leadership,* 73(8): 36–42.

Schneider Jack. 2014. *From the Ivory Tower to the Schoolhouse: How Scholarship Becomes Common Knowledge in Education.* Cambridge, MA: Harvard Education Press.